■Citizens
and Society

POLITICAL LITERACY TEACHER RESOURCE PACK

TED HUDDLESTON

INDIVIDUALS
ENGAGING IN
SOCIETY

Citizenship Foundation

Hodder Murray

A MEMBER OF THE HODDER HEADLINE GROUP

This resource pack is the result of a two-year curriculum development project run by the Citizenship Foundation with funding from the Department for Education and Skills, and evaluated by Ian Davies and Sylvia Hogarth, University of York.

The author is grateful to the members of the project advisory group for their encouragement and support during the development period:

Jonathan Blundell, Judith Church, David Claydon, Anna Douglas, Barry Dufour, Ruth Kerry, Will Ord and Gabby Rowberry.

Grateful thanks are also due to the many individuals who gave their time to help pilot and evaluate draft materials or lent their support in different ways, in particular to the teachers and students of the following schools and colleges:

Batley High School; Bemrose School, Derby; Biddenham Upper School, Bedford; Broxtowe College, Chilwell; Caldew School, Carlisle; The Cedars Upper School and Community College, Leighton Buzzard; Crawshaw School, Pudsey; Crompton House School, Oldham; De Aston School, Market Rasen; Derby Moor Community School, Derby; Dr Worrall Special School, Sheffield; Hartland School, Worksop; Harton School, South Shields; Heanor Gate School, Derbyshire; Huntington School, York; Ilkley Grammar School; Keswick School; Kingsmead Support Services, Derby; Langdon School, London; Lees Brook Community School, Derby; Littleover Community School, Derby; Morpeth School, Tower Hamlets; Southlands High School, Chorley; St Bede's School, Lytham St Annes; Thistley Hough High School, Stoke-on-Trent; Whitby Community College; Whitley Bay High School; Wilson's School, Wallington; Wycombe High School, High Wycombe.

Special thanks are due to Don Rowe for his wise counsel on occasions too numerous to mention.

The publishers would like to thank the following individuals, institutions and companies for permission to reproduce copyright illustrations in this book:

© CORBIS 101; © Bettman/CORBIS 146, 147; © Chris Bland, Eye Ubiquitous/CORBIS 53; © PA photos 140; © Durand Patrick/CORBIS SYGMA 91; © Reuters/CORBIS 21, 60, 139; © Ferdaus Shamim/CORBIS 130.

The publishers would also like to thank the following for permission to reproduce material in this book:

The Citizenship Foundation 131; *Evening Press*, York 21; The *Guardian* 82, 83; The *Independent* 52; www.kelkoo.co.uk 75; *Market Research News* 36; The *Milton Keynes Citizen* 152; *The Times* 28.

Every effort has been made to trace and acknowledge ownership of copyright. The publishers will be glad to make suitable arrangements with any copyright holders whom it has not been possible to contact.

Artwork by Simon Rumble at Beehive Illustrations.

Papers used in this book are natural, renewable and recyclable products. They are made from wood grown in sustainable forests. The logging and manufacturing processes conform to the environmental regulations of the country of origin.

Note about the Internet links in the book. The user should be aware that URLs or web addresses change regularly. Every effort has been made to ensure the accuracy of the URLs provided in this book on going to press. It is inevitable, however, that some will change. It is sometimes possible to find a relocated web page, by just typing in the address of the home page for a website in the URL window of your browser.

Orders: please contact Bookpoint Ltd, 130 Milton Park, Abingdon, Oxon OX14 4SB. Telephone: (44) 01235 827720. Fax: (44) 01235 400454. Lines are open from 9.00–5.00, Monday to Saturday, with a 24 hour message answering service. You can also order through our website www.hodderheadline.co.uk.

British Library Cataloguing in Publication Data
A catalogue record for this title is available from the British Library

ISBN 978 0 340 81241 9

First published 2004
Impression number   10 9 8 7 6 5 4 3 2
Year   2008

Copyright © Citizenship Foundation 2004

Cover photos © Picture Net/Corbis; © Associated Press
Typeset by Phoenix Photosetting, Chatham, Kent
Printed in Great Britain for Hodder Murray, an imprint of Hodder Education, part of Hachette Livre UK, 338 Euston Road, London NW1 3BH by Hobbs the Printers Ltd., Totton, Hampshire

CONTENTS

ABOUT THIS PACK

Who it is for

Citizens and Society is a resource pack to support the teaching of political literacy in schools and colleges.

It has been developed by the Citizenship Foundation as part of a two-year project funded by the Department for Education and Skills and tested in a range of schools across the country.

The pack is intended for teachers of Citizenship working with older students in Key Stage 3, Key Stage 4 and beyond. It has particular application for those preparing students for examination in GCSE (Short Course) Citizenship Studies and GCE AS Social Studies: Citizenship, and will also be found useful in GCE AS Government and Politics and Critical Thinking, and in General Studies and Key Skills.

What it seeks to achieve

Citizens and Society does not set out to be another factual survey of the institutions and processes of the British political system, nor is it primarily concerned with thinking about or debating the future of this system. Rather it seeks:

to introduce young people in a systematic way to the sort of ideas and arguments that make political thought and debate possible.

It starts from the premise that politics is essentially controversial and that in order to understand political issues, young people need to be familiar with the beliefs and values that lie behind them. They also need to be familiar with the vocabulary in which political thought and argument take place.

This sort of *conceptual* approach to political literacy is very much in its infancy in schools and colleges. For this reason, there is included in this introduction a brief outline of the nature of politics and political literacy, and some of the types of teaching strategy that make for effective learning in the classroom.

USING THE MATERIALS

Teaching units

The pack is divided into 16 separate teaching units. Each unit focuses on a central question in political debate, and introduces students to some of the key concepts and vocabulary that enable them to explore the question in depth and evaluate the different ways in which people have tried to answer it.

The teaching units are set out in the form of outline lesson plans, each containing enough work for a minimum of one hour's work in the classroom.

Aims and objectives

Each teaching unit begins with specific learning objectives,

capable of objective assessment at the end of the unit if required.

In addition to specified learning outcomes, every teaching unit is intended to contribute to the development of students' skills of political enquiry and communication. In particular, they provide practice for students in:

- thinking about and researching topical political issues
- analysing political information from different sources
- expressing, justifying and defending personal opinions on political issues orally and in writing
- contributing to group and exploratory discussions on political issues, and taking part in debates
- using their imagination to consider other people's experiences and evaluating political views that are not their own.

Citizenship themes and concepts

Each teaching unit is mapped onto the requirements of the 'knowledge and understanding' strand of the National Curriculum programme of study for Citizenship at Key Stages 3 and 4. Coverage is indicated in the 'Citizenship themes' section at the beginning of each unit, and in the diagram in Figure 2, pviii. Each of the teaching units also introduces the learner to a different set of political concepts (see Figure 2, pviii).

Background notes

It is possible to feel overwhelmed by the sheer complexity of ideas and arguments that surround the subject of politics. In principle, however, politics is no more complex than any other area of human interest and concern. That it might seem so may be explained by reference to the historical lack of political education within the English school curriculum. It is important that teachers do not feel they have to be experts in political philosophy to use this pack. The teachers' notes in the 'Background' section near the beginning of each teaching unit should provide enough basic information to get started.

Keywords

Language learning is an important aspect of political literacy, and in recognition of this a list of important words and phrases is included in each of the teaching units. These lists are for guidance only. They indicate the kind of terminology that might usefully be introduced in each topic.

The lesson

Each lesson is divided into a number of key sections: starter activities, the main lesson, plenary and research tasks. Interspersed throughout the text of the different sections are additional teachers' notes of a more practical nature (indicated by a tinted box), including tips and hints for classroom use, suggested answers, alternative ways of introducing topics, and guidance on how to set up particular learning activities in the classroom.

1. Starter activities

Starter activities are brief introductory exercises designed to focus student interest and attention on the topic to be explored and some of the key issues it raises. They are also useful for establishing students' prior learning in the area with which it deals and enable the teacher to pitch work and judge the pace of the lesson more appropriately.

2. The main lesson

The focal point of each lesson is a piece of stimulus material, such as a story, hypothetical scenario, or dialogue, incorporating in a concrete situation the relevant political issues to be explored. Students engage with the stimulus material, gradually unpacking the issues it involves, through a number of role-play, problem-solving or discussion activities. Photocopiable stimulus material, activity sheets and writing frames needed in the lesson are printed at the end of each unit.

The basic structure is provided by a series of questions. The questions have been carefully chosen to focus student enquiry on the issues most central to the unit and can be answered either orally or in writing. Teachers are requested to stick as closely to the questions as they can, although it is recognised that a modicum of rewording may be necessary in some cases.

3. The plenary

The lesson itself ends with a short plenary activity to summarise and reinforce key learning points. It also provides the teacher with an opportunity for assessing student levels of interest and progress, and for evaluating the success, or otherwise, of the lesson as a basis for future planning.

4. Research tasks

The research tasks at the end of each unit are designed to help students apply their learning to real-life, topical issues – locally, nationally and internationally. These tasks can be used in different ways: as extension work, homework assignments, or ideas for the Citizenship 'activity', or coursework, component of the GCSE (Short Course) Citizenship Studies examination.

Planning a course

The teaching units in *Citizens and Society* have been constructed so as to be usable either singly or in groups and in almost any order. However, they are much more likely to be effective when grouped together, or linked to other Citizenship activities, in the form of short modules. To help teachers do this, the units have been grouped into four different topics:

1. Citizens

2. Society

3. Government

4. Politics.

Broadly speaking, within each of these topics, the material becomes progressively more challenging from unit to unit. For teachers with little curriculum time to spare, the first unit in each topic would make an ideal initial introduction to political literacy.

Citizenship studies and other external examinations

Citizens and Society will be found particularly useful by teachers preparing students for the GCSE (Short Course) in Citizenship Studies and for GCE AS Social Science: Citizenship. For a diagram mapping out the relevant teaching units for the different awarding bodies, see Figure 1, pvii.

The teaching units also make useful introductory lessons for GCE AS Government and Politics, and provide content for the AS examination in Critical Thinking, as well as for Key Skills and General Studies. In fact, the sort of concept-based, enquiry-driven approach adopted in the pack is ideally suited to the development of critical thinking skills at all levels.

■ *POLITICS AND POLITICAL LITERACY*

What is politics?

Politics can be defined in many different ways. In general terms, politics is the process by which a group of people with different opinions or interests reaches collective decisions about the way their life together should be organised. It involves persuasion and negotiation, and some kind of mechanism for reaching a final decision, e.g. voting. It also involves power and authority, and an element of coercion – if only to ensure that collective decisions are made binding on the group as a whole.

On this definition, any social institution – the school, the football club, even the family – has its own 'politics'.

Politics within a Citizenship context

In *Citizens and Society*, however, we are primarily concerned with politics within the context of *democratic citizenship*. In this sense, politics is defined primarily in terms of the *institutions of state* and the *relation between a state and its citizens.*

The focus is on the public dimension of life in society and the part that citizens should play in it – their rights and responsibilities. We are concerned with questions such as: where should political power lie, and how should it be wielded? How should decisions affecting the running of the country be taken, and who should take them? What makes a society a fair one?

Democratic politics is not just about voting. It is also about discussion and debate, and opportunities for citizens to make their voices heard on issues of public importance. For this reason, public debate has an essential part to play in the definition of politics used in this pack.

What is political literacy?

Political literacy is sometimes defined as *effectiveness in public life*. Effectiveness implies some sort of ability or capacity. It does not necessarily mean participation as such. In a democracy, schools and colleges have a right – more properly, a duty – to help students develop the capacity to participate effectively in public life, but that is as far as the mandate goes. They have no right to dictate how, or even whether, they should participate.

So what does a citizen need to be effective in public life? At least three things are required:

- conceptual understanding: of political ideas and arguments, beliefs and values
- factual information: about the political system and how it works – locally, nationally and internationally
- practical skills: of political participation and action.

We can think of these as the three, inter-related 'strands' of political literacy.

In *Citizens and Society*, we are first and foremost concerned with the first of these – though elements of the other two strands are necessarily covered from time to time. This is because it is conceptual understanding that binds the three strands together. Conceptual understanding allows people to make sense of and discuss the political system. Without it, knowledge about civic institutions and processes remains a mere collection of inert facts. Conceptual understanding makes it possible for citizens to reflect upon their motivations for wishing to change society – or maintain the *status quo* – and their choice of methods for trying to do so. Without critical reflection, political action degenerates into mindless activism.

Conceptual learning is central to political literacy and, in recognition of this, each of the teaching units in this pack introduces the learner to a different set of political concepts – see Figure 2, pviii.

■ STRATEGIES FOR TEACHING AND LEARNING

Enquiry-based learning

The approach to political literacy teaching adopted in this pack owes much to the idea of 'enquiry-based' learning. Although didactic forms of teaching and learning have a role to play, especially in the introduction of political knowledge, much more is to be gained by *engaging learners personally* in the issues they are studying and providing them with opportunities to develop and express their own opinions.

One way of doing this is through *discussion and debate*. Talk is central to the teaching and learning process in political literacy for several reasons: first, it helps to stimulate thinking; second, political problems are social problems and social problems are best explored through dialogue; and third, the ability to engage in debate on issues of political consequence is a prerequisite for participation in a democratic society.

For discussion to take place – in the classroom, as anywhere else – there has to be something to discuss. This is why *active learning* is important. The experience of involvement in active learning activities, such as role-play, improvisation or simulation exercises, provides the raw material for discussion work. *Story* works in a similar way. Stories are rich in possibilities and engage learners in a variety of ways – emotionally and intellectually. By teasing out the various political elements embedded in a narrative, young people are able to build up a more sophisticated knowledge of politics and political issues.

This is not to diminish the importance of *written work*, however. Written work has many different uses in the political literacy lesson. It is both a way of recording thoughts and a stimulus to thought itself – a good way of encouraging personal reflection. The ability to express political opinion and argument in writing is one of the aims of the Citizenship programme of study for Key Stages 3 and 4. Most of the key questions posed in the teaching units in this pack are capable of being answered in writing as well as orally.

Ground rules

Successful discussion work depends upon the acceptance of ground rules, e.g. not speaking when others are speaking, not making fun of others, etc. It is important, therefore, that students are:

- aware of what the rules are
- understand why they are there
- know they will be enforced.

Teachers may wish to establish the ground rules at the beginning of a course. Alternatively, students can be encouraged to negotiate the rules for themselves.

Seating arrangements

It is essential that students are able to see and hear each other comfortably. It is helpful to have the option of two or three different seating arrangements that students are able to move between quickly and with relative ease, each one conducive to a different form of discussion or learning activity. Where there are large numbers in a class, a double-horseshoe formation with space at one end for the teacher can be particularly effective.

The classroom as a public forum

Used in this way, the classroom becomes a kind of model public forum in which students practise political discussion and debate as a kind of rehearsal for adult life. Each group of young people has the characteristics of a pluralist society in miniature. It is made up of different individuals from different backgrounds, espousing different political beliefs and values, all sharing membership of a common institution and having a common identity.

However, students are not simply citizens-in-waiting; in important ways, even if under 18, they are citizens in their own right. For this reason, the Citizenship classroom should be seen not only as a model public forum but also as an *actual* one. For many young people, the classroom is the first sort of public forum they experience and provides the first opportunity they have to debate issues of political concern as citizens for real.

■ ASSESSING POLITICAL LITERACY

Forms of assessment

The assessment of learning is as important an aspect of political literacy teaching as it is in any area of Citizenship, or any other school or college subject. As elsewhere, the form the assessment should take depends upon the circumstances, in particular upon:

- the needs of the students
- the purpose of the assessment.

To help students and teachers gain an impression of student progress, for example, a brief test completed in pairs at the end of a lesson may be sufficient. A five-minute debrief in which students reflect publicly on the quality of debate in the lesson, the main arguments voiced, and so on, can serve the same purpose. For more detailed information on individuals' strengths and weaknesses, a short written self-assessment might be more appropriate, with a tick-box schedule for less confident writers. Where assessment is part of an externally accredited examination, e.g. GCSE (Short Course) Citizenship Studies, something more rigorous will be appropriate.

Areas of assessment

The form the assessment should take also depends upon the area of political literacy learning that is being assessed. As far as GCSE and GCE AS levels are concerned, the areas for assessment are set out in the published specification of the awarding bodies.

For National Curriculum Key Stages 3 and 4 work, the areas to be assessed are set out in the programme of study. They are:

- knowledge and understanding about becoming informed citizens
- skills of enquiry and communication
- skills of participation and responsible action.

The programme of study insists, however, that Citizenship teaching should ensure that knowledge and understanding are acquired and applied 'when developing' skills. This implies that, as far as the assessment of political literacy is concerned, skills should not be divorced from subject matter. So, for example, one is expected to assess not simply a student's ability to take part in debates, but to take part in *political* debates. What is required from the student is not simply confidence in public speaking, but confidence in speaking publicly about *political* issues. This is why *Citizens and Society* places so much emphasis on student familiarity with political ideas, arguments, beliefs and values.

Figure 1
GCSE (Short Course) Citizenship Studies

Awarding body	Topic/theme	Relevant teaching units
AQA	Topic 1c Local Community	6, 8
	Topic 2a National and European Government	1, 2, 3, 4, 12, 13, 16
	Topic 2b Criminal and Civil Law	5, 7
	Topic 2c The Media	14, 15
Edexcel	Theme 1: Communities and Identities	4, 6, 8
	Roles and Responsibilities	1, 3, 7, 13
	Criminal and Civil Justice	5
	Theme 2: Power and Politics	2, 10, 11, 12, 16
	The Media	14, 15
	Theme 3: Global Business	9
OCR	Theme 1: Citizenship – Rights and Responsibilities	1, 4, 5, 6, 7, 8, 9, 14, 15
	Theme 2: Citizenship and Government	2, 3, 10, 12, 16
	Theme 3: Citizenship and Participation	2, 13

GCE AS Social Science: Citizenship

Awarding body	Topic/theme	Relevant teaching units
AQA	Module 1: The Citizen and the State	1, 3, 4, 5, 13
	Module 2: The Citizen and the Political Process	2, 10, 11, 12, 16
	Module 3: The Citizen, Society and the Community	6, 7, 8, 14, 15

Figure 2

Unit	Title	Citizenship programme of study	Key concepts
1	What does it mean to be a citizen?	Legal and human rights and responsibilities Central and local government Diversity of national, regional, religious and ethnic identities	Citizenship Rights Responsibilities Identity
2	How can we make politicians listen?	Opportunities to bring about social change Playing an active part in democratic processes The importance of resolving conflict fairly	Protest Pressure group Identity
3	Why pay taxes?	Public services and how they are financed How the economy functions Central and local government	Taxation Redistribution The economy Public services
4	Why should we love our country?	Diversity of national, regional, religious and ethnic identities Legal and human rights and responsibilities The importance of resolving conflict fairly	Patriotism National identity Diversity
5	Should we be free to do what we want?	Legal and human rights and responsibilities The importance of resolving conflict fairly Aspects of the criminal justice system	Freedom Civil liberties Human rights Rule of law
6	What makes a society a fair one?	Legal and human rights and responsibilities Central and local government Diversity of national, regional, religious and ethnic identities	Social justice Class Hierarchy Minority rights Socialisation
7	Is equality always fair?	Legal and human rights and responsibilities Central and local government Diversity of national, regional, religious and ethnic identities Public services and how they are financed	Social equality Discrimination Life chances Equal opportunities
8	How tolerant should we be?	Diversity of national, regional, religious and ethnic identities Legal and human rights and responsibilities The importance of a free press	Tolerance Mutual respect Pluralism Inclusion
9	Is free trade fair trade?	How the economy functions Rights and responsibilities of consumers, employers and employees Legal and human rights and responsibilities	Free market Capitalism Interventionism
10	Why do we need a government?	Central and local government Parliamentary and other forms of government Public services and how they are financed	Government State Power Authority Common good
11	What is the best way to run a country?	Parliamentary and other forms of government The electoral system and the importance of voting	Government Democracy Monarchy Theocracy Dictatorship
12	How can everyone have an equal say?	The electoral system and the importance of voting Parliamentary and other forms of government Legal and human rights and responsibilities	Democracy Representation Parliament Electoral reform Constitution
13	What should the state do for us?	Public services and how they are financed The work of voluntary groups	Welfare state Social rights Public services Individual responsibility
14	What makes a good politician?	Central and local government The media's role in society Public services and how they are financed The rights and responsibilities of consumers	Public interest Accountability Freedom of information Pragmatism
15	Why won't politicians answer the question?	The media's role in society Central and local government	The media Rhetoric Oratory Propaganda Public opinion
16	What do political parties stand for?	Central and local government Parliamentary and other forms of government Legal and human rights and responsibilities	Political parties Ideology Liberalism Conservatism Socialism

Citizens

▨ AIMS

This unit aims to help students to:

- know what a citizen is

- understand how someone becomes a citizen of the UK

- consider the sort of rights and responsibilities that UK citizens should have.

▨ CITIZENSHIP THEMES

- Legal and human rights and responsibilities

- Central and local government

- Diversity of national, regional, religious and ethnic identities

▨ KEYWORDS

absolute rights	rights that should never be taken away from people
alienation	feeling that you do not belong
citizen	member of a state with legal rights and responsibilities
citizenship	(1) membership of a state with legal rights and responsibilities
	(2) taking an active part in the community
conditional rights	rights that have to be earned
human rights	rights all people should have whatever society they belong to
social exclusion	not having the same rights and opportunities as other citizens, being left out of society

▨ BACKGROUND

This is a unit about citizenship. A citizen is a member of a state with a legally defined set of rights and responsibilities. How a person becomes a citizen varies from state to state.

Anyone born in the UK before 1 January 1983 is automatically a British citizen. If you were born in the UK on or after this date you are a British citizen by birth if either of your parents are British citizens or they are entitled to live

here permanently. If your parents are not married, only your mother's position counts.

Becoming a British citizen by naturalisation or registration depends upon a number of factors, such as if you marry a British citizen, how long you have lived here, if you are permanently settled here (or intend to remain here permanently), and if you are of 'good character'.

This is a complicated process. The current law will be found in the British Nationality Act 1981 and the Nationality, Immigration and Asylum Act 2002. For more information, visit the Home Office's website at *www.homeoffice.gov.uk*

For specialist advice, ask at your local Citizen's Advice Bureau.

As the way in which a person is granted the status of citizenship varies from state to state, so do the legal rights and responsibilities that go with this status. What should these rights and responsibilities be? In the context of a democratic society, at least five types of right are said to be involved. They are:

civil rights	=	the freedom to do what you like with your life, e.g. freedom of speech, freedom of movement
political rights	=	the right to have your say about the way society is governed, e.g. to vote in elections, stand for political office
social rights	=	access to a reasonable standard of living, e.g. welfare benefits, medical care
cultural rights	=	the right to join in activities that people in your society enjoy or benefit from, e.g. to go to university, have access to art and music
environmental rights	=	the right to live in a healthy environment, e.g. to breathe clean air, drink clean water.

What these rights entail in practice is a matter for debate. Citizens may have different opinions. What is not in dispute is that whatever rights go with membership of society, all citizens should be able to receive them in equal measure, e.g. the right to equal treatment from the law and equal access to the law. But is this really the case in this country? In practice, people can be excluded on account of their family background, education, class, gender or ethnicity.

The central activity in this unit is a poem, or 'rant', by someone who feels he is being treated like a second-class citizen. He is from a poor family, has no qualifications and no job. He is therefore unable to afford many of the things that other people take for granted, e.g. a car, a computer and foreign holidays. He feels discriminated against by the law and feels that he has no voice in the society in which, formally at least, he is a citizen. To make matters worse, he is constantly told that this 'second-class' status is his own fault.

This raises a number of important questions. What sorts of rights should all citizens enjoy? Why are certain citizens denied access to these, and what should be done about it?

What sort of responsibilities do all citizens have? Are citizens rights absolute, or are they conditional on citizens first fulfilling these responsibilities, e.g. should citizens forgo social security benefits if they do not make enough effort to find work themselves?

Unit 1 WHAT DOES IT MEAN TO BE A CITIZEN?

■ INTRODUCTION

This is a lesson about citizenship. In this lesson, you will learn what a citizen is, how someone becomes a citizen of the UK, and about the sort of rights and responsibilities that UK citizens should have.

■ STARTER

How does someone become a British citizen? Is it do with:

■ where you are born?
■ who your parents are?
■ filling in an application form?

As you will see from the background information on p2, each of the answers has some truth in it, but needs to be qualified.

■ SECOND-CLASS CITIZEN

Read **Second-class citizen** (Student Sheet 1.1, p6). You may wish to perform this as a 'rant'.

1. In pairs, reflect upon these two questions.

■ How is the writer feeling?
■ Who does the writer blame for this?

Suggested answers	
THE WRITER FEELS:	THE WRITER BLAMES:
▪ *angry*	▪ *people who criticise him*
▪ *frustrated*	▪ *people who will not listen*
▪ *left out*	▪ *people who look down on him*
▪ *unfairly treated*	▪ *people who have the advantages he does not*
▪ *ignored*	▪ *society in general*
▪ *looked down on*	▪ *politicians.*
▪ *discriminated against.*	

2. Share your answers with the class.

3. In small groups, think about your response to this. Look at the words on the Discussion Cards (Student Sheet 1.2, p7). Choose the ones that most closely reflect what you, as a group, would want to say to the writer. Develop some arguments to support your choice.

4. Compare your group's ideas with the class.

5. In your groups, think about the sort of rights the writer thinks he is entitled to from society. You may wish to note down your thinking on Student Sheet 1.3, p8.

■ How many different ones can you find? Draw up a list.

<table>
<tr><td colspan="2" align="center">Suggested answers</td></tr>
<tr><td>
• *to a job*
• *to social/leisure facilities*
• *to respect*
• *to be listened to*
• *to equal treatment by the law*
• *to a clean environment*
</td><td>
• *to be able to fulfil his potential*
• *to holidays abroad*
• *to a 'flashy' car*
• *to his own computer*
• *to his own flat.*
</td></tr>
</table>

■ Which of these rights do you think it is fair for someone to expect from society?

■ Which of them do you think it is unfair to expect? Why? Discuss your answers with the class.

6. Together, consider what citizens should have to do to get their rights. Do you think the country should expect something from citizens in return for the rights they are given? If so, what?

<table>
<tr><td align="center">Suggested answers</td></tr>
<tr><td>
YES:
• *respect the law*
• *respect other citizens*
• *respect the government*
• *be proud of their country*
• *work hard*
• *put something back.*

NO:
• *citizens are simply entitled to their rights and that is all there is to it.*
</td></tr>
</table>

■ PLENARY

On your own, reflect upon what you think is the most important right that *all* citizens should have in this country and why. Write down your answer, then go round the class and compare everyone's ideas.

☆ □ SECOND-CLASS CITIZEN

I'M A SECOND-CLASS CITIZEN
CITIZEN
WHY DON'T YA LISTEN
LISTEN?

They say, 'Get a job,
It's the making of you' –
I got no exams,
So what can I do?

They say, 'Join a club' –
Okay, okay,
You tell me a club
That's not miles away.

They say, 'Keep your nose clean' –
But that's not ee-zee
When there's one law for them
And another law for me.

They say, 'Do your bit,
Jump up and take part' –
When I say what I think,
They say, 'Son, depart.'

I'M A SECOND-CLASS CITIZEN
CITIZEN
WHY DON'T YA LISTEN
LISTEN?

Have a holiday in the sun,
Drive a flash-ee car,
Jacuzzi bath when day is done,
Brand new comput-a.

YEH, RIGHT, YEH, RIGHT.

Move into a trend-ee flat,
Do a Maths degree,
Mummy, Daddy pay ya way
Thru' uni-versi-tee.

YEH, RIGHT, YEH, RIGHT.

Fresh air blowing on ya face,
Trampin' in the country;
Everywhere clean 'n' bright,
Green 'n' rubbish-free.

YEH, RIGHT, YEH, RIGHT.

Form a boyband, do wah-wah,
Star in West End play,
Winning goal for QPR,
Dance in the ball-ay.

YEH, RIGHT, YEH, RIGHT.

They say, 'It's your duty,
There's no saying "pass",'
They say, 'You don't like it,
You get off your ass.'

They say, 'Love your count-ree,
The Queen is your mother.'
Didn't ask to be born here,
So why should I bother?

They say, 'Vote for us,
We're simply the best.'
But when it ends up,
They're just like the rest.

They say, 'Take an interest,'
But I'd like to see
One of them ✱✱✱✱✱✱s
Take an interest in me.

I'M A SECOND-CLASS CITIZEN,
WHY DON'T YA... LISTEN
LISTEN!

☐ DISCUSSION CARDS

Take more pride in yourself.	Make a bit more of an effort. You only get out of life what you put in.
If you don't like this country, why don't you go and live somewhere else?	You don't need exams to succeed in life.
Count yourself lucky. What about all those starving people in other countries?	It would be boring if everyone were alike.
You deserve better.	We can't all be sports stars or sing in boybands.
Do not give up.	Do not be so ungrateful.
You are just as good as them.	I know how you feel.
Moaning will not do any good.	Something else…?

☆ ☐ CITIZENS' RIGHTS

Rights	Fair to expect	Unfair to expect

☐ RESEARCH TASKS

■ CITIZENS' DUTIES

What sort of duties does the British state demand of all its citizens? Think about the following responsibilities. Choose two or three and find out whether they are required by law from ALL/SOME/NO British citizens. Explain your findings to the class.

- Paying tax
- Voting in elections
- Jury service
- Swearing loyalty to the Queen
- Registering to vote in elections

- Defending the country in the event of war
- Trying to get a job
- Carrying an identity card
- Reporting crime.

■ SECOND-CLASS CITIZENS IN YOUR COMMUNITY

1. What groups of people do you think are treated like second-class citizens in the community in which you live?

2. Think of some examples.

3. Choose one that you feel strongly about.

4. Find other people in your class who also feel strongly about this.

5. Together, collect some evidence on the group you have chosen to study, e.g. from newspaper articles, the Internet, interviews, surveys.

6. Prepare a presentation about your chosen group. Explain how you think this group is being left out of society and what you think should be done about it.

7. Invite in someone from the local community who you would like to be present for your presentation, e.g. local councillor, police officer, community leader, MP, youth worker, businessman/woman.

■ AIMS

This unit aims to help students to:

■ become familiar with different forms of political protest

■ learn about their advantages and disadvantages

■ consider when, if at all, civil disobedience can be justified.

■ CITIZENSHIP THEMES

■ Opportunities to bring about social change

■ Playing an active part in democratic processes

■ The importance of resolving conflict fairly

■ KEY WORDS

activist	person much involved in campaigning for a cause or for a political party or pressure group
campaign	activity, or series of activities, designed to make a change in society
civil disobedience	form of protest that involves deliberately breaking the law
demonstration	form of public protest, e.g. a march
direct action	form of protest that involves action rather than words, e.g. obstructing the building of a road
hunger strike	form of protest that involves refusing to eat or drink
lobby	try to influence or win the support of influential people
petition	written statement people sign as a way of showing their support for a campaign
policy	a plan of action
political party	group of people with a particular set of political beliefs, formed to elect people to government
pressure group	group of people formed to campaign on a particular issue
surgery	time when an MP, or local councillor, is available to meet the people he or she represents

■ BACKGROUND

This unit is about political protest. Conventionally, political action involves joining or supporting political parties and voting or even standing as a candidate in elections. This form of action is best applied to causes that are general and non-urgent. Where a cause is particularly urgent, or more specific or local, or where a course of action decided upon by elected representatives is basically unjust, alternatives to the ballot box may be more appropriate, e.g. campaigns, marches, demonstrations.

Extra-parliamentary action is often, though not always, co-ordinated by 'pressure groups'. Pressure groups exist to exert pressure or influence on elected representatives. They provide alternative views to those expressed by political parties and a range of different means by which citizens can take part in the political process.

Under articles 10 and 11 of the European Convention of Human Rights, incorporated in UK law through the Human Rights Act, everyone has the right to freedom of peaceful assembly and to freedom of association with others, including the right to form and join trade unions, for the protection of their interests. These are not absolute rights, of course. Governments are entitled to restrict these where the restriction is 'necessary in a democratic society'.

While there is general agreement about the function of extra-parliamentary action in a democracy, what is more controversial is the kind of tactics that are used – from letters and websites to obstructing the public, causing damage to property, or even endangering lives. Just because a particular tactic is effective, does not mean it is morally right. So which sorts of campaigning can be justified and which sorts cannot? To a certain extent, this must depend upon the circumstances. So in what kind of circumstances, if any, is civil disobedience justified?

Gandhi identified several principles in which civil disobedience might be justified. These include the following:

■ based on respect for the law

■ non-violent

■ done in public

■ protesters accept their full punishment

■ after all other attempts have failed

■ a matter of urgency, e.g. danger to human life.

As is often the case, it is the practical application of the principles that is controversial. What starts out as non-violent protest may not always end up that way.

There are no minimum age limits on organising or signing petitions, talking or writing to an MP or local councillor, writing letters to the press, taking part in a radio or TV phone-in, attending meetings of your local council, or taking part in marches and demonstrations. Political activities that do have minimum age limits include:

- join a trade union (16)

- vote in general and local elections (18)

- stand for public office, as a local councillor, MP or MEP (21).

Rules for joining political parties vary. There is no age limit for membership of the Conservative and Liberal Democratic parties, but you need to be 15 to join the Labour Party.

The central activity in this unit is about two young people who become involved in a campaign to prevent a school friend from being deported. In the process, they explore a number of different forms of protest, from petitions to public demonstrations. They also have to deal with criticism that what they are doing is pointless or simply inappropriate for young people of their age. As the story continues, however, the stakes are raised. They have to decide whether to go on with the campaign in the face of death threats and the possibility that they will now be breaking the law.

The story raises a number of questions. Is civil disobedience ever justified? What sacrifices must a citizen be prepared to make in order to secure the welfare of fellow citizens? What forms of political protest are open to young people who are not old enough to vote?

Unit 2 HOW CAN WE MAKE POLITICIANS LISTEN?

■ INTRODUCTION

This is a lesson about political action. In this lesson, you will learn about different forms of political action, about their advantages and disadvantages, and whether you think that it is ever right to break the law to make the government listen.

■ STARTER

Imagine you were being driven mad by pollution and noise from heavy lorries in your neighbourhood. How far would you be prepared to go to try to stop them? Why? You may wish to note down your thinking on Student Sheet 2.1, p14. Discuss your answers with the class.

■ KARL MUST STAY!

Read the story **Karl must stay!** (Student Sheet 2.2, pp15–16).

1. In small groups, think about the sorts of argument the parents could use to try to persuade Robin and Nikki not to go.

Suggested answers

- *it is too dangerous*
- *you will get into trouble with the police*
- *you should stop to think about your family*
- *it will not stop Karl being sent away if you do go*
- *Karl is not your responsibility*
- *it is the law – you have no right to question it*
- *you have not stood up for other people who have been deported*
- *you have got more important things to do, like schoolwork*
- *you are too young to understand all the issues*
- *the way to change the law is by voting in elections.*

Make a note of your ideas on Student Sheet 2.3, p17.

2. How do you think Robin and Nikki could respond to these arguments?

> ### Suggested answers
>
> - *we can look after ourselves*
> - *we have come so far, we cannot stop now*
> - *we owe it to Karl – he is our friend*
> - *our presence might make all the difference*
> - *it is important enough to make it worth the risk*
> - *it is a matter of principle*
> - *somebody has to make a stand*
> - *young people have wider responsibilities than just to their families*
> - *young people have to stand up for young people*
> - *citizens have a duty to make a stand against injustice*
> - *Karl would have stuck up for us if it had been the other way round*
> - *we are too young to vote, so we are taking the only form of action that is available to us*
> - *by the time of the next election, Karl will have gone*
> - *the law is not always right.*

Make a note of your ideas on Student Sheet 2.3, p17.

3. Improvise a conversation in which Robin and Nikki's parents are trying to persuade them not to go to the demonstration at the town hall.

4. Think about the arguments you have used. Do you think it is right for citizens to break the law just because they feel strongly about an issue? If not, why not? If so, under what circumstances?

5. In your group, think about the different sorts of political action that citizens could use. Consider each one in turn and decide what its main advantages and disadvantages are. You may wish to note down your thinking on Student Sheet 2.4, pp18–19.

6. Discuss your answers with the class.

■ *PLENARY*

Take a class vote on whether you think Robin and Nikki should go to the demonstration. What, for you, is the most important factor in making this decision? Ask around the class and compare your views on this. Of all the points made – except your own – which one are you most impressed by?

> You may wish to label opposite ends of the room 'YES' and 'NO' and ask students to vote by going to the end that most closely matches their feelings – with a section for 'STILL NOT SURE' in the middle.

☐ HOW FAR WOULD YOU GO?

Imagine you were being driven mad by pollution and noise from heavy lorries in your neighbourhood. How far would you be prepared to go to try to stop them?

Think about the following actions and tick the ones you would be prepared to do if you had to.

Sign a petition ☐

Go on a march ☐

Ring the council ☐

Complain to the owner ☐

Lie down in the road to prevent the lorries passing ☐

Damage the lorries in some way ☐

Something even more drastic? ☐

Where would you draw the line and why?

_____

_____

_____

_____

☐ KARL MUST STAY!

The trouble started when Karl's father left. The authorities said that with his father gone, Karl and his mother had no right to stay in the UK any more. They would have to leave.

Karl was one of the most popular students in his class — with the other students, that is. He was tall for his age and good looking. His friends liked him because he was a good laugh and always stood up to the teachers if there was any trouble. They did not want him to go. Anyway, it was unfair they thought: being sent away to another country where he would have no friends and could not even speak the language. It was not as if he had done anything wrong.

So Robin and Nikki asked their form teacher what they could do. The form teacher said it was not really anything to do with them. It was the law and that was all there was to it.

Then Nikki heard that people who worked with Karl's mum had formed a support group. They were signing a petition to allow her to stay in this country. They had been told at the local law centre that it might be possible to let Karl and his mum stay on 'compassionate grounds'.

This gave Nikki and Robin an idea. They got some paper and a clipboard and went round their school asking for signatures. Some people signed; others just laughed and told them they were wasting their time.

Then, out of the blue, a reporter from the local newspaper arrived at their school. She was writing a feature about racism. There had been a number of racially motivated attacks on newcomers to the town recently.

Two days later Nikki, Robin and Karl appeared on the front page of the local newspaper. By the side of the article was a piece by a local councillor criticising Nikki and Robin for getting up their petition. He said that children at secondary school were too young to get involved in politics. They did not understand what they were doing and could well do more harm than good.

This only encouraged Nikki and Robin more. They made a banner and hung it from the school gates. It said:

KARL MUST STAY!

This was too much for their head teacher. She called them into her office and told them the protest was giving the school a bad name and it would have to stop. If it did not, she might have to consider suspending them.

That weekend, the support group for Karl's mum planned a big demonstration outside the town hall. But the police banned them from holding it. They were worried about troublemakers coming from out of town and someone getting seriously hurt. That did not stop the organisers, though. They said the demonstration would go ahead as planned, whether they were breaking the law or not.

Then something else happened that Robin and Nikki had not bargained for. Someone sprayed graffiti on the front walls of their homes. It read:

Would they be as keen to go to the demonstration now...?

☐ ARGUMENTS AND COUNTER-ARGUMENTS

Arguments the parents could use	How Robin and Nikki could respond

☐ POLITICAL ACTION

Think about the following sorts of political action. Consider each one in turn and decide what you think its main advantages and disadvantages are.

Action	Advantage	Disadvantage
Voting		
Writing to newspapers		
Organising a march		
Ringing the council		
Setting up a website		

Joining a political party	Direct action	Publicity stunts	Speaking to your MP	Organising a petition	Running an advertising campaign	Taking part in a phone-in	Other?

☐ RESEARCH TASK 1

■ *PRESSURE GROUPS*

Pressure groups are groups of people who get together to influence or put pressure on the government or people in a position of authority. It is a form of political action that people can use when voting does not work, or is too slow, or when political parties do not seem to be interested in the issues that other citizens think are important.

Broadly speaking, there are two main types:

sectional groups: who stand up for people in particular jobs or professions, e.g. trade unions

cause groups: who promote particular beliefs or attitudes, e.g. Child Poverty Action Group.

1. Find out which sort of pressure group each of the following is. Is it a 'sectional' group, a 'cause' group, or a mixture of both? Explain your answer.

- Greenpeace
- British Medical Association
- Countryside Alliance
- CND

- Liberty
- Animal Liberation Front
- Shelter
- Confederation of British Industry

2. Find out which pressure groups there are in your local community. They could be local groups such as a tenants' association, or a local branch of a national group such as Amnesty International or MIND. Your local library is a good place to start.

3. Choose a pressure group that you and your friends are interested in and research what it does. Make sure you include:

- its purpose
- the sort of tactics it uses
- how it is funded.

Make a presentation on the group you have chosen. You may wish to invite in a representative from the group to help with the presentation or answer questions.

☐ RESEARCH TASK 2

■ *PUPILS STAGE ANTI-WAR PROTEST*

Police were called to a school in York after hundreds of students protesting against the war with Iraq spilled out onto the city streets.

Four students aged between 14 and 16 were excluded from Joseph Rowntree School for two days for 'inappropriate behaviour' during the demonstration.

This followed a day of protest by York school students when dozens of young people walked out of Fulford School and All Saints School to march into the city.

City of York education chief, Patrick Scott, said the safety of students was 'paramount'.

He said: 'It's a very different situation if students demonstrate on school grounds rather than spill out onto the public roads where their safety is clearly at risk.'

Head teacher Hugh Porter said that the four students were excluded for their behaviour, not for taking part in the protest.

Student Tim Johnson, 16, said: 'It was a protest against a war with Iraq and the teachers were trying to stop us from doing it.'

Reproduced courtesy of Evening Press, York

1. Write a short piece expressing what you think about the issues raised by this incident. Try to answer the following two questions:
   - ■ Were the pupils right to protest in this way?
   - ■ Was the punishment a fair one?

2. Conduct a survey into whether people think secondary school students should be allowed to go on protests during lesson time.

Think carefully about:
   - ■ who you are going to ask – just young people or a cross section of people?
   - ■ how you are going to record their views – questionnaire, interview, or other?
   - ■ how you are going to present the findings – written report, video, etc?

For information about the law and student protest, go to *www.citizenshipfoundation.org.uk*

■ AIMS

This unit aims to help students to:

■ identify different forms of taxation

■ recognise the advantages and disadvantages of different forms of taxation

■ learn how taxation can be used to affect social and environmental change.

■ CITIZENSHIP THEMES

■ Public services and how they are financed

■ How the economy functions

■ Central and local government

■ KEYWORDS

council tax	a tax paid to the council by home-owners or tenants, based on the value of the property they live in
fiscal	to do with the way a government raises and spends money, especially in connection with tax
hypothecation	a specific tax to pay for a specific service, e.g. a penny on income tax for education
progressive tax	a tax where the rate increases as the amount being taxed increases
public services	services needed by the community as a whole, e.g. street lighting, education, waste disposal, social services
redistribution	sharing out on a more equal basis
regressive tax	a tax where the rate decreases as the amount being taxed increases
revenue	income, money coming in
tax	compulsory payment collected from citizens to raise money for government spending
tax burden	amount of money people are required to pay in tax

■ BACKGROUND

This unit is about taxation. Taxation is the chief source of government revenue in the UK. The money raised from taxation is spent largely on public services, e.g. education, defence, transport, social security, housing, law and order; but also in other ways such as international aid or in the form of interest on public borrowing. Decisions about taxation are taken by the Government, i.e. by the Prime Minister and the Cabinet, through the Chancellor of the Exchequer. The Government draws up a budget each year in which it decides the amount it needs to spend and how it will raise that money.

Taxation can take different forms. It can be direct or indirect. Direct taxes are paid by individuals or organisations, e.g. income tax, National Insurance. The government department responsible for assessing and collecting this type of tax is the Inland Revenue. Indirect taxes are taxes charged on the goods and services we buy, e.g. value added tax (VAT), fuel tax. They are collected on behalf of Customs and Excise by the person or company selling them. Although the range of taxes that citizens pay is decided by central government, certain taxes are set and collected locally, e.g. council tax, business rates.

Although most taxes go towards general government spending, there are some that are earmarked for particular purposes. The money raised by National Insurance, for instance, is used to provide citizens with income at certain times when they are unable to work – in the form of incapacity benefit and maternity benefit, retirement pensions, job seeker's allowance, etc. Similarly, council tax is used to pay for local council spending.

Which citizens should pay tax and how much should they pay? These have been longstanding questions in political debate. One view is that all citizens should pay as everyone benefits from public services. Against this, many would argue that some people simply do not have the money, so tax liability should to some extent be based on the ability to pay. Should everyone pay the same or should some pay more than others? One view is that those who can spare the most should pay the most. But others might say that high levels of taxation stifle both wealth creation, lessening the overall sum available to spend on public services and charitable giving. Should taxation be used just to raise income needed for public spending or ought it be used for other purposes? In the UK, taxation has often been seen as a way of encouraging or discouraging certain forms of behaviour, e.g. smoking, car use, marriage. More controversially, it is also seen as a mechanism for ensuring a more equal distribution of wealth throughout society, evening up inequalities in income due to accident or heredity.

The central activity in this unit concerns members of a youth club who, unable to find any other source of funding, decide to pay for the new equipment they want out of their own pockets. They agree that each should pay a weekly sum out of their pocket money and part-time earnings until the club has what it needs – in other words, a kind of voluntary income tax. This raises the questions: what are the most practical ways of doing this, and which is the fairest?

■ INTRODUCTION

This is a lesson about tax. In this lesson, you will learn about different kinds of tax, why we have them, and what you think is the fairest way of taxing people.

■ STARTER

Test yourself

To test your knowledge about tax, divide into small groups and look at the items on the Discussion Cards (Student Sheet 3.1, p25). Which of these things do you think people in the UK have to pay tax on? Which do you think are tax-free? Divide the cards into two piles: TAXED and NOT TAXED.

There is no tax on bread, children's clothes or magazines. However:

- Customs and Excise duty is payable on cigarettes, alcohol and petrol

- the interest on savings is subject to income tax if you earn or receive income over a certain amount each year

- retirement pensions are subject to income tax if you earn or receive income over a certain amount each year

- National Insurance is paid on the wages people are paid – over a threshold of £89 per week – and wages are also subject to income tax if you earn or receive income over £4615 each year

- stamp duty is payable if you buy a house above £60,000; council tax is based on house value and is charged to house-owners and tenants; if you sell a house that is not your main residence, you could be liable to capital gains tax

- Customs and Excise duty is payable on new cars, and car repairs are subject to VAT

- personal stereos and adult clothing are sold with VAT included in the selling price.

With the exception of retirement pensions, young people, in principle at least, are subject to all these forms of taxation.

Tax rates correct January 2004.

■ MELBURY YOUTH CLUB

To help you understand more about tax, read **Melbury Youth Club** (Student Sheet 3.2, p26).

1. In small groups, think about the objections the club members make to Lena's suggestion. How could Lena answer these objections? Look at each one in turn and think of what Lena could say to make them change their minds. You may wish to note down your thinking on Student Sheet 3.3, p27.

2. Share your ideas with the class.

3. Imagine the club members agree to pay for the new facilities in this way. In small groups, consider the kind of system they will need. What do you think is the fairest way of organising this?

■ ISSUES TO THINK ABOUT INCLUDE:

- Should everyone have to pay the same amount or should some be expected to pay more than others?
- What should be done about someone who refuses to pay?
- What should be done about people who cannot really afford to pay anything?
- How should they decide what the money raised is to be spent on?
- When should payments be due?
- Who should be responsible for looking after the money they raise?

You may wish to ask students to think of the relevant issues for themselves, e.g. what sorts of things the club members will need to think about, rather than present them with a ready-made list of points to consider.

4. Present your ideas to the class for discussion.

■ PLENARY

Reflect upon what you have learned from the Melbury Youth Club exercise. What sort of things do you think people can learn about taxation in real life from doing an exercise like this? Write down all the different things you can think of, then choose two or three of your points to share with others in your class.

☐ DISCUSSION CARDS

Cigarettes	**Bread**
Pensions	**Petrol**
Alcohol	**Clothes**
Cars	**Wages**
Houses	**Magazines**
Savings	**Personal stereo**

☐ MELBURY YOUTH CLUB

Young people at the Melbury Youth Club are discussing the state of the room where the club meet three nights a week. The pool table has been vandalised and several of the balls are missing. The table-tennis table will not stand up properly. There is nothing to play music on, no games to play, nowhere to make a drink, and hardly a seat fit to sit on.

They tried to apply a grant from the council, but the council had no money. They have tried holding car-boot sales, but have never had much luck. If they held car-boot sales for the next ten years, they would still not have enough money to pay for the facilities they want at the club.

So Lena makes a suggestion:

'I've got an idea. Why don't we pay for the improvements ourselves? We all get pocket money, have part-time jobs, or get paid for helping at home. If we all pay a certain amount from what we get paid each week, like a kind of income tax, we'll have enough money to get what we need for the club in next to no time. What do you say?'

This is how some of the others respond:

☐ WHAT COULD LENA SAY?

Think about the objections the club members make to Lena's suggestion. How could Lena answer these objections? Look at each one in turn and think of what Lena could say to make them change their minds.

■ Why should we pay? Other kids could just come along and get the benefit of the new facilities for free.

> Lena could say:

■ I've got my own pool table at home. Why I should have to pay for another one?

> Lena could say:

■ Why should my mates and I have to pay? We only come to the club for a laugh, anyway. If we really want to enjoy ourselves, we get the bus into town.

> Lena could say:

■ I'm going off to university in a couple of months' time. Why should I pay for something I'm not going to get that much use out of? If anyone should pay, it should be Tom. He's loaded. He's got wealthy parents. It's about time he was made to share some of his money with the rest of us.

> Lena could say:

■ I'm hopeless at pool. So why should I pay for a new pool table? I might consider it if it were for a new sound system, but not for a pool table.

> Lena could say:

■ If I had to pay for things for the club out of my paper round, I'd give up my paper round there and then. What would be the point of getting up at the crack of dawn every morning for next to nothing?

> Lena could say:

☐ RESEARCH TASK 1

■ BURGER TAX 'WOULD CUT OBESITY'

A tax on fat should be imposed on hamburgers to help to tackle the increase in obesity in Britain, according to a leading nutritionist.

Mo Malek, of St Andrews University, says that fatty fast food, which is now an established part of the nation's diet, could be a health hazard as serious as cigarettes in ten years' time. The number of people classified as obese in Britain has doubled in the past 15 years to 15 per cent of the population, about one in six adults.

Professor Malek argues that the Government should intervene and use the tactics it employs to discourage smoking. Heavy taxes on fatty foods would force people to improve their diets. He wants the government to put a 10p tax on burgers, with the highest levy on the most fatty product.

'The Government needs to do two things. It must encourage us to eat less and one way to do it is to put VAT on fatty foods. At the same time, that should force companies to compete with each other more on quality, rather than quantity.'

Treating obesity and illnesses linked to it, such as heat disease, stroke, cancer and diabetes, already costs the NHS an estimated £3.5 billion a year.

Professor Malek claims that a typical burger meal at a fast-food restaurant contains up to 60 per cent fat. 'Companies like McDonald's or Burger King will say their burgers only contain ten per cent or 15 per cent fat, but the meal is not just the burger. There is also the processed cheese, the mayonnaise and ketchup, and the French fries,' he said. 'All that fat lodges in the arteries.'

A Burger King spokesman said yesterday: 'The idea of fast-food customers being penalised for enjoying a burger once a week seems very unfair.'

The Times, 9 October 2002

1. What are the pros and cons of a burger tax? Generate some arguments for and against putting VAT on fatty foods.

2. Governments sometimes use taxation to try to alter people's behaviour, e.g. putting a tax on cigarettes to try to stop people smoking. Do you think this is a good idea? Why or why not? If you do, what other items do you think should be taxed in this way? Why?

3. Find out how much tax there is to pay on:

   ■ a packet of cigarettes
   ■ a pint of beer
   ■ a bottle of wine
   ■ a litre of petrol

You can find this on HM Customs and Excise website: *www.hmce.gov.uk*

4. There is a view that says that we should use the tax system to make society more equal. The idea is that by setting high rates of tax for wealthy people and low rates for the not-so-wealthy, we will all become more equal in the long run. This is known as 'redistribution'. What is your opinion of using taxation in this way?

☐ RESEARCH TASK 2

■ *COUNCIL TAX*

Council tax is a tax paid on the house or flat where you live. The amount of tax you pay is set every year according to the value of your property. Each house is fitted into a band, A–H, according to how much it will sell for. The bands are the same across the country, but the local council sets the amount payable in each band. If you live in a rented house or flat, you pay council tax as if you owned the property.

This means that the amount of council tax someone has to pay in, say, Devon, may be quite different from the amount paid by someone living in a similar house in Manchester. It also means two people living in the same kind of house in the same area have to pay the same amount of council tax, even if one is much richer than the other.

1. Do you think that council tax is a fair tax? Why or why not? If you think it is unfair, can you think of a fairer way in which local councils could raise money?

2. Find out how much council tax people with houses in bands A–H have to pay in your area.

3. Find out how much council tax a person has to pay if they have more than one home.

4. Education is a local council's most costly service. Some people who pay to send their children to private schools think it is unfair to expect them also to pay tax for education. They say they are paying twice over for their children's education – once in school fees and once in tax. Do you think it is fair to expect them to do this? Why or why not?

For information about council tax in your area, go to your local council's website. For information about the amount of council tax paid on a specific house, go to *www.upmystreet.com*

AIMS

This unit aims to help students to:

- reflect upon reasons why people may not wish to be patriotic

- learn about ways in which people can be encouraged to become more patriotic

- consider the role of patriotism in a democratic society.

CITIZENSHIP THEMES

- Diversity of national, regional, religious and ethnic identities

- Legal and human rights and responsibilities

- The importance of resolving conflict fairly

KEYWORDS

diversity	made up of different kinds
jingoism	boasting about the superiority of your own country over others
national identity	image that citizens of a state have of themselves
nationalism	(1) a very strong, or exaggerated, sense of devotion to your country (2) political belief that all nations should govern themselves
nationality	being a citizen of a particular country with legal rights and responsibilities
patriotism	a feeling of love for your own country
pluralism	belief in the value of forms of society in which different cultures, religions and ethnic groups can live together on an equal basis
xenophobia	fear of strangers and of things foreign

BACKGROUND

This unit is about patriotism. The love of one's own country has traditionally been thought of as an important value in a healthy and cohesive society. It motivates citizens to put aside their own selfish interests in the interests of the good of society as a whole and develop a sense of community. For some people, patriotism is thought of as a duty owed by citizens to the state in return for everything the state does for them.

However, love of one's country need not always be a positive thing. It can spill over into xenophobia, racism or militant nationalism. It can also reinforce difference and injustice within society. This is because patriotism often involves a form of national self-consciousness, an awareness of separate identity by a nation. It is how this sense of national identity is defined that is the significant thing.

National identity may be defined in many different ways. On the one hand, it can be defined in terms of a particular skin colour, ethnicity, religion, language, place of birth or type of character. On the other hand, it can be defined in terms of attitudes and values, e.g. fair play, tolerance, a commitment to diversity and democracy, etc. The question is not whether loving your country is a good thing, but what sort of sense of national identity goes with that love. Is it rooted, for example, in notions of racial superiority and difference or in ideals such as tolerance and equality?

In the UK context, debates about patriotism revolve around ideas about 'Britishness' and what it is to be British. For various reasons, many UK citizens do not always wish to identify themselves as British – as a result of discrimination or social exclusion, or because of the way that in this country patriotism has sometimes been hi-jacked by groups with racist agendas. It is also because people have the possibility of multiple identities. We can identify ourselves in terms of our families and friends, religion, ethnicity or region we belong to – even in terms of the world or planet as whole – as well as in terms of the state or states where we possess citizenship. Conflicts of loyalty can arise between these different forms of self-identification.

The central activity in this unit is a questionnaire evaluating different ways in which we might encourage citizens in this country to become more patriotic. It raises a number of important questions. What does it mean to love one's country? Is it a good thing to love one's country regardless of what the country is like or stands for? Can you love your country too much?

WHY SHOULD WE LOVE OUR COUNTRY? Unit 4

■ *INTRODUCTION*

This is a lesson about patriotism. In this lesson, you will learn reasons why people do not always love their country, things that can be done to encourage people to love their country more, and how important you think it is for citizens to love their country.

■ *STARTER*

Hated ring tones

A survey showed that the British national anthem, God Save the Queen, is the most hated ring tone on mobile phones. One in four people said they could not bear to hear the national anthem on a mobile. Other patriotic tunes, Rule Britannia and Three Lions, were also among the most hated.

Survey by phone insurance group CPP, 2003

- Think about why people hate these tunes so much. What different reasons can you think of?
- Share your ideas with the class.

■ *PATRIOTISM*

1. As a class, think of reasons why someone might dislike their own country. How many different reasons can you think of?

> ### Suggested answers
>
> - *think other countries are better*
> - *came from another country and would prefer to return but cannot*
> - *feel badly treated by the country*
> - *do not feel a part of the country*
> - *think the quality of life in their country is not as good as it should be*
> - *think life in their country is unfair*
> - *think the country is being run badly*
> - *disagree with what the country is doing to/in other countries*
> - *disagree with something the country did in the past*
> - *have stronger loyalties elsewhere, e.g. to region, religion, local community.*

2. In small groups, consider what sorts of thing would be likely to make citizens of this country love Britain more. Fill in the questionnaire (Student Sheet 4.1, pp33–34).

3. Present your answers to the class and discuss the points you disagree over.

4. In small groups, decide what you think 'loving your country' should mean. How can you tell when a person loves their country? Draw up a list of some of the kinds of thing you would expect a patriotic citizen to do.

Suggested answers

- *go to war to defend their country*
- *support national sports teams*
- *sing the national anthem*
- *support/speak out for national institutions, e.g. the monarchy*
- *fly/wear the Union Jack*
- *insist on speaking English abroad*
- *participate in national politics, e.g. vote*
- *do voluntary work*
- *try to make their country a fairer place*
- *buy British goods.*

6. As a class, consider the following questions.

■ Do you think it is a good thing for citizens to love their country? Why or why not?

Suggested answers

YES:
- *they are more likely to do things for it, help others, etc.*
- *it can help hold the country together at a time of crisis*
- *citizens have a duty to love their country because of all their country does for them*

NO:
- *it leads to hatred of people from other countries*
- *it means people are too easily satisfied with things that are wrong with their country and unwilling to change them*
- *it makes people less likely to accept refugees and asylum seekers.*

■ Do you think it is possible for someone to love their country too much? If so, how?

■ *PLENARY*

On your own, reflect upon your feelings at the end of this lesson. Do you feel more or less patriotic than you did earlier or are your feelings unchanged? Go round the class and compare where you stand.

☐ QUESTIONNAIRE

Study the following items. For each one, decide whether you think it would be LIKELY or UNLIKELY to make British people love their country more.

Develop some arguments to support your decisions.

	Likely/ unlikely	Reason
A new national anthem		
Better weather		
More national holidays		
Lessons in patriotism at school		
A more equal society		
Less crime		
The Union Jack on public buildings		
A British national football team		

	Likely/ unlikely	Reason
A better health service		
Armed invasion by another country		
A national awards scheme for patriotism		
Less racism		
More teaching of Christianity in schools		
England winning the World Cup		
More emphasis on British history in schools		
Cheaper holidays abroad		
Getting rid of the royal family		
Leaving the European Union		

☐ RESEARCH TASK 1

■ *STATUES IN TRAFALGAR SQUARE*

The mayor of London, Ken Livingstone, announced that he wanted to get rid of two statues in Trafalgar Square. They were statues of two British generals: Sir Charles Napier and Sir Henry Havelock.

The mayor said he wanted to get rid of the statues not only because no one today had heard of them, but also because they are not very good examples of what it means to be British.

Napier was a soldier and administrator who led troops in the conquest of the area of Sindh, in what is now Pakistan, killing 5,000 Indian troops in one day alone. Havelock, another soldier, helped to put down rebellion against British rule in India.

Critics of Ken Livingstone said Napier and Havelock were national heroes and that what he was doing in trying to get rid of their statues was destroying British identity in London.

1. Do you think Ken Livingstone was being unpatriotic in suggesting that these statues be got rid of? What are the arguments for and against this?

2. Look at the different public figures that are commemorated in statues in the area where you live. How many different ones can you find? In your opinion, are these good role models for young people today? Why or why not?

3. Carry out your own survey of what people think it means to be 'British'. What sort of people do they think should be held up as national heroes today? Why?

☐ RESEARCH TASK 2

■ *CONSUMER PATRIOTISM*

Consumer patriotism is showing loyalty to your country by buying goods and services from your country rather from abroad.

According to a survey by Roy Morgan Research, consumer patriotism is strong in Australia, somewhat less strong in the US and New Zealand, and weak in the UK.

It emerged that 74 per cent of Australians try to buy products made in their own country, while the same is true of 62 per cent of Americans, 58 per cent of New Zealanders and only 45 per cent of British people.

Asked whether they like to take holidays in their own country, 82 per cent of Australians, 80 per cent of New Zealanders and 68 per cent of Americans say they do, while the UK figure is only 57 per cent.

In all four countries, slightly more women than men are patriotic consumers. Also, in all four countries, consumer patriotism appears to increase with age.

Market Research News, 21 November 2003

1. How can you explain the relatively low level of consumer patriotism in the UK? What reasons can you think of?

2. Do you think British citizens have a duty, where possible, to buy things made in this country? What are the arguments for and against this?

3. Carry out your own investigation to test the idea that patriotism increases with age in this country. Decide how you are going to collect and present your information.

Society

■ AIMS

This unit aims to help students to:

- identify different forms of freedom

- recognise situations in which different forms of freedom conflict with each other or with other values

- learn about the different forms of freedom that are important in a democratic society.

■ CITIZENSHIP THEMES

- Legal and human rights and responsibilities

- The importance of resolving conflict fairly

- Aspects of the criminal justice system.

■ KEYWORDS

civil liberties	freedoms that all members of a society should have without interference from the government
human rights	rights and freedoms that all human beings should have whatever society they live in
libertarianism	belief that citizens should be free to live exactly as they choose providing they are not actively harming other people
liberty	freedom
'nanny state'	a government that is too protective of its citizens and does not allow people enough freedom to make their own decisions
paternalism	when someone in a position of authority decides what is best for people instead of letting people decide for themselves
rule of law	principle that every citizen of a society, no matter how important or powerful, must follow the law
vigilantes	citizens who take it upon themselves to make or enforce laws instead of leaving it to the proper authorities

■ BACKGROUND

This unit is about freedom. Freedom is one of the central concepts in political thinking. It is also one of the most contested.

This is because there are many different forms of freedom and different forms of freedom can conflict, e.g. one person's freedom to smoke may conflict with another person's freedom to breathe unpolluted air. Different forms of freedom can also conflict with other social and political values, e.g. one person's freedom to buy private medical treatment may, some might argue, conflict with another person's right to equal access to medical care.

Different forms of freedom can be classified in different ways. One way is to distinguish between negative and positive freedom. Negative freedom is the freedom to do whatever you want, without anyone trying to stop you. Positive freedom is the freedom to do the things that are worth doing in life, e.g. fulfilling your potential, having a say in the running of your society.

Alternatively, you may wish to distinguish between freedom 'to' and freedom 'from'. Freedom 'to' relates to personal choice. Freedom 'from' relates to the removal of factors that restrict your personal choice, e.g. freedom from poverty or from discrimination.

Another way is to distinguish between 'human rights' and 'civil liberties'. Human rights are the rights people are entitled to simply by virtue of being human. These are often thought of as absolute and are presumed to be the same whatever society you live in. Civil liberties are freedoms people are entitled to by virtue of being citizens of a particular society. They are defined by the needs and make-up of a particular society at a particular time and can vary from society to society. All societies recognise that there may be times when civil liberties have to be suspended or restricted on behalf of the greater good of the community, e.g. during war, national emergencies, etc.

The kind of civil liberties that have traditionally been thought to be important in UK society include:

freedom of speech	=	freedom to express, publish and broadcast opinions and views on things
freedom of movement	=	freedom to move around the country
freedom of association	=	freedom to form groups and hold meetings
freedom of conscience	=	freedom to hold beliefs and opinions on things, including religion
freedom of the person	=	freedom from arbitrary arrest.

Achieving the right balance between different forms of freedom in society is one of the enduring problems of political life. To some extent, this is a question of law. The law exists, partly at least, to guarantee citizens their essential freedoms. This is one reason why the principle of the 'rule of law' is central to the idea of a democratic society. This principle says that decisions affecting the public life of society should always be subject to the constraints and procedures of the law and that no citizen should be above the law.

The central activity in this unit concerns a group of local vigilantes trying to crack down on youth crime on a council estate. In trying to free their estate of crime, however, the vigilantes are in danger of compromising other, more basic, freedoms. This raises the questions, what sorts of freedom are important in a society and how are these best balanced against each other?

Unit 5 SHOULD WE BE FREE TO DO WHAT WE WANT?

■ INTRODUCTION

This is a lesson about freedom. In this lesson, you will learn about different forms of freedom, about how different forms of freedom can conflict, and about the different forms of freedom that are important in a democratic society.

■ STARTER

> **Robinson Crusoe** was a character in a story by Daniel Defoe, shipwrecked on a desert island off the coast of South America. The island was totally uninhabited and Robinson Crusoe found himself completely alone. He had no means of escape and little hope of being rescued. His only possessions were the few supplies that had floated ashore from his sunken ship.

> **Alfred Dreyfus** was a French army officer wrongly accused of being a spy and sentenced to life imprisonment on Devil's Island. Devil's Island was a prison colony built on barren rock off the coast of South America. When Dreyfus arrived, the island was cleared of people except for him and his guards. He was given a stone hut 13 feet square to live in and 200 yards of space for exercise. If he tried to escape he would be shot.

- Which of these two men do you think had the most freedom? Why?
- What different kinds of freedom are there? Which do you think are the most important? Why?

■ CHERRY LEA'S ANGELS

To help you think about freedom in society, look at the **Warning!!!** poster (Student Sheet 5.1, p42).

1. In pairs, think about the poster from Cherry Lea's Angels' point of view. What do you think Cherry Lea's Angels mean when they say they want the estate to be 'free'? What kind of freedoms do you think they have in mind? How many different ones can you think of?

Suggested answers

FREEDOM:
- *from misery*
- *from fear*
- *from vandalism*
- *from violence*
- *from muggings*
- *from having their homes broken into*
- *from graffiti*
- *from drug dealers*
- *from a feeling of helplessness*
- *to walk the streets in safety.*

2. Now think about the poster from the point of view of the young people living on the estate.

■ Do you think what Cherry Lea's Angels are going to do is likely to restrict young people's freedom in any way?

■ If so, what kinds of freedom will they restrict? How?

Suggested answers

FREEDOM:
- *to go out in groups of more than two*
- *to meet with friends*
- *to go into pubs or shops*
- *to have a say about what happens on the estate*
- *to be listened to*
- *to be considered innocent until proven guilty*
- *to live on the estate*
- *to buy alcohol*
- *to walk the streets in safety*
- *from harassment*
- *from discrimination.*

3. Share your ideas with the rest of the class.

4. As a class, think about the actions Cherry Lea's Angels are taking. Do you think the residents of an estate should be free to protect themselves in this way? Why or why not?

Suggested answers

YES:
- *they have a right to protect themselves*
- *no one else will do it*
- *if all the proper channels have failed*

NO:
- *it might get out of hand and go too far*
- *there is no one to check whether they are acting fairly*
- *there are proper channels to go through, e.g. council, police*
- *what would happen if everyone took the law into their own hands?*

5. On your own, think about the kinds of freedom that are important in society. Draw up a list of the kinds of freedom that you think are most important. Make a note of the ones that, in your view, should in no circumstances be taken away from a person.

6. Share your ideas with the rest of the class. Explain the thinking behind your choice.

■ PLENARY

As a class, see if you can agree on one aspect of life in this country where there should be more freedom for citizens and one aspect of life where you think freedom should be restricted.

⚠ WARNING!!!

We're sick and tired of the way you **young thugs** have been allowed to make the lives of people on this estate a complete misery – with all your vandalism, graffiti, fighting, drug dealing, and robberies.

All the politicians do is talk and make empty promises. The police either cannot be bothered to do anything or are just too plain sh*t scared to show their faces.

So we, the residents of the Cherry Lea estate, have decided to do something about it ourselves.

We are forming a residents' protection group. We are called **'Cherry Lea's Angels'**. Look out for the combat gear and red 'CLA' armbands.

AS FROM NEXT WEEK, WE WILL BE PATROLLING THE ESTATE ON A REGULAR BASIS.

1. **Youths hanging round in groups of two or more will automatically be moved on.**

2. **Anyone acting suspiciously will be searched for weapons, drugs and alcohol.**

3. **All weapons, drugs and alcohol will be confiscated.**

4. **Anyone damaging property will be made to pay for it.**

5. **Drug dealers and thieves will be given 24 hours to get out of the estate – or else!!**

6. **The names of all other troublemakers will be put on a list which will go up in all shops, pubs, etc. If your name is on the list, do not expect to get served! We will see to that.**

WE WILL NOT REST UNTIL THE RESIDENTS OF THIS ESTATE ARE FREE!!!

□ RESEARCH TASK 1

■ *THE HUMAN RIGHTS ACT*

A group of European countries came together in 1949 to form the Council of Europe. They were determined never to let the horrors of the Second World War happen again. The Council of Europe drew up a list of basic rights and freedoms that all European citizens ought to be able to enjoy. This list became known as the European Convention of Human Rights.

The Council of Europe also set up the European Court of Human Rights to which citizens of any of the Council's member states can go if they think their rights or freedoms under the Convention are being violated.

In 1998, the UK Parliament passed the Human Rights Act. The Act, which came into full force in 2000, made the Convention's most basic rights and freedoms part of UK law. For the first time in this country, considering every citizen's human rights has become a central part of our law. It is the UK government's responsibility to make sure that all British citizens are able to enjoy these rights.

1. What basic rights and freedoms are dealt with in the Human Rights Act?

2. The Human Rights Act only applies to 'public authorities'. What counts as a 'public authority'? Can you list some examples? What does this aspect of the Act mean for the ordinary citizen?

3. If you think one of your freedoms under the Act is being violated, what can you do about it?

4. Under the European Convention, governments of member states are allowed to suspend or restrict certain rights and freedoms during a public emergency. This is known as 'derogation'. Can you find an example of a government doing this?

For information on the Human Rights Act, useful websites include:

■ *www.lcd.gov.uk/hract*
■ *www.citizenshipfoundation.org.uk*

☐ RESEARCH TASK 2

■ ANTI-SOCIAL BEHAVIOUR ORDERS (ASBOS)

An ASBO is a form of punishment given to someone who has been involved in serious anti-social behaviour on a number of occasions. You do not actually have to commit a crime to get one: offensive behaviour or repeated verbal abuse of a neighbour can be enough. ASBOs last for a minimum of two years and may be given to anyone aged ten or over.

Manchester City Council has recently produced leaflets telling local people about children and young people on ASBOs in their area. The leaflets are in full colour and contain photographs and details of the children and young people concerned. They set out the 'offences' the young person has committed and explain why the order has been made.

If the young person is banned from a certain area, the leaflet contains a street map showing where they are not supposed to go. Some of the leaflets include newspaper articles relating to the case, e.g. 'Unmasked, the girl gang leader', or 'The tormentor aged 13'.

Some people think that the leaflets violate young people's civil liberties. Others disagree, arguing that the leaflets are a good way of cutting youth crime.

1. What are the different arguments for and against using leaflets like these? How many can you find?

2. Normally, the media are not allowed to identify young people who are given a punishment by a magistrates' court. But they are allowed to do so in this case because an ASBO is a 'civil' order not a 'criminal' one. What is the difference between a 'civil' and a 'criminal' order?

3. Carry out your own investigation into a complaint about civil liberties being violated. Find out the different freedoms that are involved and explain whether or not you think the complaint is a fair one.

Examples you might choose to include:

- ■ Identity cards
- ■ CCTV
- ■ The Anti-Terrorism, Crime and Security Act 2001.

■ AIMS

This unit aims to help students to:

■ become familiar with different ideas of social justice

■ learn about the sorts of thing that makes a society a fair one

■ reflect upon issues of social justice in this country.

■ CITIZENSHIP THEMES

■ Legal and human rights and responsibilities

■ Central and local government

■ Diversity of national, regional, religious and ethnic identities

■ KEYWORDS

hereditary principle	principle that advantages in society can be passed down through the family from one generation to the next, e.g. wealth, power, property
hierarchical	arranged in different levels or grades
meritocracy	society that rewards people who use their talents and work hard
paternalism	when a government or people in authority decide what is best for people instead of allowing people to choose for themselves
self-determination	ability to choose how to live your own life
social class	a group of people who share a similar position in society on account of income, status, occupation or access to power
social justice	fairness in society
status quo	existing arrangement or state of affairs

■ BACKGROUND

This unit is about social justice. Social justice is concerned with the just society. Achieving a just, or at least a less unjust, society is the ultimate aim of all political thought and action. It is about achieving a fair distribution throughout society of the kinds of benefits and burdens that living in society can bring, e.g. property, wealth, political power.

What makes a society a fair one has been a recurrent question in Western thought. Different political ideologies have offered different theories of social justice. Historically, four major criteria determining the fairness of the distribution of social benefits and burdens have been:

■ tradition

■ equality

■ merit

■ need.

The idea of *tradition* dictates that society should operate in the same way as it always has done, and that a fair society is one that respects traditional forms of organisation and ways of doing things. So, if you live in a hierarchical society and accept this view, your idea of a fair society will be one that is hierarchically organised with different grades of citizen allotted different rights and freedoms.

Those who value *equality* believe that each citizen deserves equal treatment on account of their equal citizenship. Equal treatment can mean different things, however. On the one hand, it can mean equality of opportunity: on the other hand, equality of outcome. The former means giving citizens the same opportunities in life, the latter means making citizen's lives the same. They are two separate principles and can sometimes conflict. Is a fair society one in which all citizens have an equal chance to get rich or one in which the gap between rich and poor is a negligible one?

Distributing social goods on the grounds of *merit* means rewarding or withholding rewards from citizens in terms of the contribution they make to society, e.g. through hard work, skill or ability. Those who contribute most deserve most. The difficulty with this in practice, of course, is determining exactly what someone's contribution to society has been. Who contributes most to the country's economy: the factory-owner or the worker on the factory floor? How can this be measured?

Those who emphasise *need* work on the assumption that all citizens have an equal right to have their basic needs satisfied irrespective of whether they deserve it or not. However, basic needs are hard to define. We agree that everyone needs food, water and shelter. But where do we draw the line? Do people need work, for example? Or cars? What is regarded as a basic need in one society may not be in another.

None of the criteria is problem free. Even if we agree about a criterion, we may disagree about how it is to be applied in practice. For example, if we agree that men and women should get equal pay for work of equal value, we may still disagree about whether particular kinds of work *are* of equal value. Nevertheless, decisions have to be taken and public policy has to be made. We may say that some or all of the four criteria of distribution are essential, but in practice we have to choose a dominant one or a regular priority between them and argue for it. That is why all citizens need to know what the alternatives are.

The central activity in this lesson revolves around an email sent by someone enjoying a weekend in a holiday cottage in the countryside. The writer extols the virtues of the sort of community life enjoyed by the people there, such as full employment, a low crime rate, cheap housing, etc., but fails to recognise that these social benefits come at a cost. The whole area is owned by one person who runs the community virtually single-handedly. Local people have little say in how their lives are run and little opportunity to better themselves. The only person who feels able to criticise these arrangements is the teacher at the village school who is a newcomer to the valley.

This raises questions about fairness in society and how a society can be made a fairer one.

WHAT MAKES A SOCIETY A FAIR ONE?

■ INTRODUCTION

This is a lesson about social justice. In this lesson, you will learn about different ideas of social justice, about what makes a society a fair one, and how fair you think society is in this country today.

■ STARTER

Which groups of people do you think are treated unfairly in this country? Draw up a list. Think of reasons to support your choice.

Suggested answers

- children
- women
- immigrants
- disabled

- poor
- ethnic minorities
- old people.

Share your ideas with the class. Which sort of unfairness does the class think is the worst? You may wish to take a vote on this.

■ HI, ANGIE!

Read the email sent from Fewdale (Student Sheet 6.1, p50).

1. As a class, brainstorm some reasons why the teacher at the village school might think life in Fewdale is unfair.
2. Discuss briefly how the person sending the email might disagree with her.
3. On your own, think about the people who live in Fewdale. Why do you think there are so few complaints about life there?

Suggested answers

- they are all happy
- they all think it is fair
- they think the disadvantages of living there are outweighed by the advantages
- it is so much a part of their lives that they do not think to question it
- they do not think anyone will listen if they do complain
- they do not have the confidence to complain
- they feel they have to keep in with the Major and do not want to 'rock the boat'

4. Why do you think they all vote for the Major in elections?

Suggested answers

- *no one else stands against him*
- *they think he is the best person for the job*
- *they have always voted for him in the past*
- *they are afraid of what might happen if the valley turns against him.*

---

5. Imagine the writer of the email meets the teacher in the village pub and the conversation comes round to the question of fairness in Fewdale. In pairs, role-play the sort of conversation you think they might have.

You may wish to ask students to write a dialogue instead of improvising a role-play.

---

6. Choose two volunteers to 'hotseat' the two characters in the role-play. Question them about their views and how they have reached them. If you are not satisfied with their answers, tell them why.

7. In small groups, reflect upon life in Fewdale for yourselves. Make a list of all the arguments for it being FAIR and all the arguments for it being UNFAIR. How many different ones can you think of? Write each one on a 'post-it' note and stick up the two sets of arguments on opposite walls of the room. Alternatively, note down your thinking on Student Sheet 6.2, p51.

Suggested answers

FAIR:
- *everyone has a job*
- *everyone knows where they stand*
- *rents are low*
- *there is no crime*
- *everyone has a home*
- *the Major has a right to do what he wants with his own property*
- *no one complains*
- *people can always leave Fewdale if they want to.*

UNFAIR:
- *one man owns the whole valley*
- *one man runs everything*
- *people feel they have to bow down to the Major*
- *people have little choice about the kind of work they do*
- *people are not able to better themselves*
- *people are not really free to complain or express their opinions*
- *the Major is very wealthy yet his workers are on low wages*
- *the Major's house is huge compared to everyone else's*
- *the Major had the chance to go to a public school when the others did not*
- *women have to work harder than the men*
- *people from outside the valley are not allowed to live there – only rent a cottage for the weekend*
- *people with different lifestyles are not welcome there*
- *people cannot own their own homes.*

---

8. Read through the different arguments in the display or ask two volunteers to do this for the class.

9. Finally, in your small groups, discuss what you think about life in Fewdale. Do you think it is fair? Why or why not? Try to reach an overall group decision and share it with the class.

■ *PLENARY*

On your own, complete the following sentence:

'A fair society is one in which…'

Then think of an example of where, in your opinion, society in this country is still unfair – something you feel strongly about. Take it in turns to read out your answers and the examples you have chosen.

☐ HI, ANGIE!

From:	m.allan@globalmail.co.uk
To:	angelaschwartz@planetnet.com
Subject:	weekend away

Hi Angie! We're having a long weekend at a holiday cottage in Fewdale.

It's unbelievable! So peaceful, and the views are outstanding! Not a bit like London. No crime. No unemployment. No homeless people.

Everyone here looks so healthy. Most of them work on farms. You should see the woman who cleans our cottage! Four kids and a husband to look after and she's out in all weathers seeing to the animals! All the farmers' wives here are the same. I don't know how they do it!

Just across from our cottage there's this huge mansion. It's enormous! The guy who lives there — Major Brown — owns the whole valley. It's been in his family for generations. We saw him in the village pub last night. All the locals stopped talking when he walked in. They're so respectful! They never use his first name (it's Iain, by the way). They just call him 'Major', and they never speak to him unless he speaks to them first.

He came up and introduced himself to us. Told us how much he loved Fewdale and its traditions, and how he missed it when he was sent off to public school as a child. He's so loyal! He won't let people from outside the valley live in any of his houses (apart from the holiday cottages, of course). He will only rent them out to his workers, even though he could get more money from someone else. Locals couldn't afford to live here otherwise — not on the wages they get!

The Major just about runs everything in Fewdale — the parish council, the church council, the school governors. Whenever there's an election for a committee, no other candidate stands a chance. He's just so popular with everyone here!

There's just one person the Major is not popular with — that's the new teacher at the village school. The Major hates her. He told us that if she were one of his farm workers, he would have sacked her by now. It is taking him longer to get rid of her because she's a teacher and he has to go through the official channels. She just doesn't fit in. She doesn't go to church. She has no respect for the traditions and way of life of the valley. She spends more time teaching the kids about racism and their rights than she does teaching them to read and write, and she is always saying how unfair it is in Fewdale. Unfair? Honestly! How ungrateful! The woman doesn't know when she's well off!

Must go, see you back in London,
luv M xxx

☐ LIFE IN FEWDALE

FAIR	UNFAIR

☐ RESEARCH TASK 1

■ FAIRNESS IN EDUCATION

Edinburgh is one of the first universities to assess students applying for places in terms of their social background.

In addition to setting a minimum requirement of three Bs at A level, Edinburgh has devised a new points system. Points will be awarded to students on such factors as:

the school they attended

■ whether anyone in the family has been to
■ university.

Credits will also be given to disabled students and those whose schooling has been disrupted by family tragedy.

Until now, Edinburgh University has had a reputation of being elitist and not recruiting enough students from poorer backgrounds.

The new system has been much criticised by top fee-paying schools. They say it is not fair to students who have worked hard at good schools for good A levels.

The Independent, 19 February 2003

1. Do you think this is a fair way of selecting students for university? Why or why not?

2. Can you think of other ways of helping more students from poorer backgrounds to get into university?

3. Do you think universities should have targets for the number of students they have to take from poorer backgrounds? Why or why not?

4. What does 'elitist' mean?

5. Some universities set admission targets for students from state (non-fee-paying) schools. Find out about a university that does this. What is the target it sets? How does it try to achieve this target? Do you think this is a fair system? Why or why not?

☆ □ RESEARCH TASK 2

■ *INHERITED PRIVILEGE?*

Some people say that one of the most important factors preventing the UK from becoming a fairer society is the way that wealth is kept within the family. People who are wealthy are not only able to provide the best for their children, but also to pass their wealth on to them when they die. The children do the same for their own children and so on.

1. Conduct a survey on whether people think it is fair that children should be able to inherit wealth from their parents instead of having to work for it themselves. You may wish to compare the views of children and parents on this issue. Record the different arguments that are used.

2. What is 'inheritance tax' and how does it work? Do you think this is a fair tax? Why or why not? You can find out about this at: *www.inlandrevenue.gov.uk*

■ AIMS

This unit aims to help students to:

■ recognise different forms of equality

■ become aware that equality sometimes means treating people the same and sometimes means treating them differently

■ learn about the forms of equality that are important in a democratic society.

■ CITIZENSHIP THEMES

■ Legal and human rights and responsibilities

■ Central and local government

■ Diversity of national, regional, religious and ethnic identities

■ Public services and how they are financed

■ KEYWORDS

discrimination	when a person or a group is treated unfairly because they are different in some way
egalitarianism	belief that every citizen has the right to receive the same benefits and advantages from society regardless of who they are or what they have done to earn them
equality of opportunity	having a chance to compete on the same terms as everyone else
equality of outcome	receiving the same benefits and advantages as everyone else
meritocracy	society that rewards people who use their talents and work hard
positive discrimination	when a disadvantaged person or group is given better opportunities than others in order to make up for their disadvantage

■ BACKGROUND

This unit is about equality. Equality is one of the central concepts in politics. It is also one of the most contested. This is because there are different forms of equality, and different forms of equality can conflict with each other or with other values.

There is a basic distinction between equality of opportunity and equality of outcome. Equality of opportunity is when people have the chance to compete on the same terms for social benefits or advantages that are limited in some way, e.g. for particular kinds of jobs or places in higher education. In contrast, equality of outcome is when everyone ends up with the same social benefits or advantages as everyone else involved, e.g. equal pay for work of equal value.

What can be confusing is that, in practice, achieving equality, whatever kind, sometimes means treating people the *same* and sometimes means treating them *differently*. Political equality, for example, is likely to mean one person, one vote, i.e. the same for all citizens, whereas achieving equality of educational opportunity usually means providing some people with special forms of education that others are not necessarily given, i.e. treating some differently from others.

Contrary to what is sometimes said, human beings are not born equal. We are born with different physical characteristics, different temperaments and different abilities. We are also born into different circumstances, some more privileged than others. This is because each society has its own in-built forms of inequality – between men and women, old and young, rich and poor, one ethnic group and another, and so on.

At least four kinds of equality have traditionally been thought to be important in the UK. They are:

equality of respect	=	idea that all human beings should be treated with the same basic respect and decency
equality under the law	=	idea that the law should be impartial and treat everyone the same regardless of birth, wealth or position in society
equal opportunities	=	idea that everyone should have the same access to the benefits and advantages that society can bring
political equality	=	idea that all citizens should have an equal say on the running of society.

The kinds of equality we value and how we think they are to be achieved depend ultimately on the sort of social and political principles we believe in. There is more to a good society than equality, and some forms of equality may not always be fair.

The central activity in this unit revolves around a story in which human beings attempt to create a world in which people are perfectly equal. As the story goes on, the characters find themselves resorting to increasingly bizarre and outlandish policies in the hope of obtaining their cherished ideal. Eventually, it becomes clear that perfect equality is neither achievable nor desirable. This is because there are different forms of equality, which have to be balanced against each other and against other values. In some cases, this means treating citizens all the same, and in others it means allowing them to be different.

This raises a number of questions. What forms of equality are important in a society? How are they best achieved? Are all forms of inequality bad? Are there forms of inequality we ought to encourage or at the very least not actively discourage?

Suggested answers to research task, Disability Discrimination Act, p61.

a. Likely to be unlawful. The swearing is a direct result of the disability so the reason for being treated less favourably relates directly to the pupil's disability.

b. Likely to be lawful, if the school is a selective one, but it will have to show that the entrance test is objective.

c. Depends. It might be possible to justify less favourable treatment on health and safety grounds, but it would be unlawful for the school to do this without first undertaking a risk assessment and considering reasonable adjustments to the weekend to accommodate the pupil.

Unit 7 IS EQUALITY ALWAYS FAIR?

INTRODUCTION

This is a lesson about equality. In this lesson, you will learn about different forms of equality, about how equality sometimes means treating people the same and sometimes means treating them differently, and about whether equality is always fair.

STARTER

The football team dilemma

The local youth club enters a five-a-side football tournament. The youth club team makes it through to the final of the tournament and eventually ends up the winner. First prize is a silver cup and five personalised football shirts with players' names on the back – all donated by a local businesswoman.

During the course of the tournament, nine different players play for the team.

■ Which of them do you think should be awarded the shirts? Why?

Suggested answers

- *the five who play in the final*
- *the five who play in the most number of rounds*
- *the five who play best overall*
- *the five who have the best disciplinary record*
- *the five who turn up for the most practice sessions*
- *the shirts should be allocated randomly*
- *no one.*

■ Which is the most equal way of awarding the shirts? Why?
■ How important do you think it is for all the players to be treated equally? Why?

DESIGNER BABIES

Read the story **Designer babies** (Student Sheet 7.1, p58).

1. In small groups, make a list of all the different things that people in the story do to try to make the world a more equal place.

Suggested answers

- *food, water, housing, hospitals, schools and elections for all*
- *random allocation of jobs*
- *banning private education and medicine*
- *redistributing wealth*
- *closing universities down*
- *uniform housing*
- *designer babies.*

2. Which of these do you think are good ideas? Why? You may wish to note down your thinking on Student Sheet 7.2, p59.

3. Which of these do you think are bad ideas? Why? You may wish to note down your thinking on Student Sheet 7.2, p59.

4. Discuss your ideas with the class. Do you think the people in the story were wrong to try to create a more equal world? Why or why not?

5. Treating people equally sometimes means treating them the same and sometimes means treating them differently. In pairs, try to think of some examples from real life to illustrate this.

Suggested answers

THE SAME:
- *the same pay for people doing the same job*
- *everyone getting one vote and only one vote*
- *the same laws should apply to everyone.*

DIFFERENT:
- *special education for people with special needs*
- *higher salaries for workers who have to live in London*
- *time off for religious holidays for people of different religions.*

6. Share your ideas with the class. Do you think all forms of equality are a good thing, or are there kinds of *in*equality that can actually benefit society? If so, what are they and how can they benefit us?

■ *PLENARY*

In your opinion, what **one** thing would most help to make the world a more equal place? Why? What do you think can be done to achieve this? Write down your ideas, then share your thinking with the class.

☐ DESIGNER BABIES

Human beings were not satisfied.

'There is too much inequality in the world,' they said. 'Some people are starving, while others have more than they can eat. Some people have no money, while others have more than they can spend. Some people do not even have a roof over their heads, while others have houses that are so big they do not know how many rooms they have got. It is not fair. Everyone should be equal.'

So human beings set about trying to create a more equal world.

The first thing they did was to share out their food equally and give everyone equal access to fresh water. Then they built houses so that everyone had somewhere to live, and hospitals and schools so that everyone could have medical care and get an education. Then they held elections and gave everyone a chance to vote.

'The world belongs to everyone,' they said. 'So it is only fair that everyone should have an equal say in the way it is run.'

Still they were not satisfied that everyone was equal. 'It is not fair that people with more money should be allowed to use it to buy better education for their children or get treated more quickly in hospital,' they said. 'Education and medical care should be equal for everyone.' So they made it against the law for anyone to run a private school or hospital, or pay for private tuition or medical treatment.

Still they were not satisfied that everyone was equal. 'Look at the huge gap between the rich and the poor,' they said. So they made a law saying that each person's money was to be added up at the end of every year. Money was then taken from those with more than average and given to those with less than average, so everyone ended up with an equal amount.

Then it was pointed out that some people were being discriminated against when they applied for a job. So to give everyone an equal chance of work, jobs were allocated at random. The person who got the job was the one whose name was drawn out of a hat first.

'That is all well and good,' they said. 'But what about university? There are not enough places for everyone who wants to go. That cannot be fair. Education should be equal for everyone.' So, as there was no money to build new universities, they closed all the old universities down.

Still they were not satisfied. 'Why should some people live in much nicer houses than others?' they asked. So they made a law saying that everyone had to move into new apartment blocks that were equal in shape, size and decoration.

Still they were not satisfied. 'It is not fair that some people are born stronger, cleverer or better looking than others,' they said. So, using the science of genetic engineering, they created a new breed of 'designer' babies that were equally strong, clever and good looking.

Eventually, everyone in the world had the same access to food; had the same access to water; was living in apartment blocks of exactly the same shape, size and decoration; went to the same type of school; was treated in the same kind of hospital; had the same amount of money, and had the same strength, intelligence and good looks.

Still, they were not satisfied. 'It is not fair that everyone should be equal,' they said. **'We want to be DIFFERENT!'**

REASONS	GOOD IDEA
REASONS	BAD IDEA

☐ RESEARCH TASK 1

■ *EQUALITY IN SPORT*

In 2003, the top prize for the winner of the women's single title at Wimbledon was £39,000 less than the men's. The winner of the men's title got £525,000, whereas the women's champion collected only £486,000. There were about half as many women's matches on the show courts as men's and a smaller percentage of television hours covering the women's game. In contrast, the top prize for women at the US Open is equal to that of men.

1. Choose two other sports and find out how men and women are treated. Do they play to the same rules? Do they compete against each other? Are they rewarded in equal terms?

2. What are the different arguments for and against treating men and women equally in sport? How many can you find?

3. Carry out an investigation into the way sport is organised for young people in your school, college or local community. Consider whether, in your opinion, girls and boys are treated equally. If you think the present system is unfair, draw up some recommendations on how you think it could be organised more fairly.

4. Conduct your own survey into whether people think men and women ought to be treated equally in sport. Think carefully about:

   ■ who you are going to ask
   ■ what you are going to ask
   ■ how you are going to record their views
   ■ how you are going to present the findings.

For information on equality for women in sport, visit the website of the Women's Sports Foundation UK at *www.wsf.org.uk*

☐ RESEARCH TASK 2

■ *DISABILITY DISCRIMINATION ACT*

Under the Disability Discrimination Act, schools and colleges are legally obliged to take reasonable steps to ensure that disabled students are not disadvantaged in any way. It is illegal for a disabled child to be treated less favourably than their able-bodied classmates unless there is a good reason for doing so.

The legal definition of disability includes 'hidden' conditions, such as mental illness and dyslexia.

Sticking to the law means much more than installing ramps and lifts, and improving wheelchair access. It also involves trips and placements, admissions procedures and the kind of education and services a student receives, e.g. schools are required by law to offer large-type worksheets to children with impaired sight.

1. Study the following situations and consider whether or not you think the schools involved were entitled to make the decisions they did. Develop some arguments to support your view.

   a. A pupil with Tourette's Syndrome is banned from a school trip for using abusive language in class. The school has a policy of banning children from trips and after-school activities if they swear or are abusive to staff. Tourette's Syndrome is a disorder that can lead to involuntary swearing or abuse; that is, the person with the disorder has no control over what they are saying.

   b. A pupil with learning difficulties is refused admission to a school because she fails an entrance test.

   c. A pupil who is a wheelchair user is not allowed to go on an outdoor activities weekend.

2. Investigate what your school or college has done, and is doing, to meet the needs of disabled students. You could start by reading the information about arrangements for disabled pupils that all schools and colleges are required to publish, and any written policies your school has on equal opportunities.

3. Find out what the Disability Rights Commission does.

■ AIMS

This unit aims to help students to:

- understand what is meant by tolerance

- become familiar with reasons why tolerance is important

- reflect upon what ought and ought not to be tolerated in a democratic society.

■ CITIZENSHIP THEMES

- Diversity of national, regional, religious and ethnic identities

- Legal and human rights and responsibilities

- The importance of a free press

■ KEYWORDS

censorship	preventing access to, or the publication of, certain sorts of information, books, films, etc.
condone	deliberately overlook or forgive something wrong
diversity	difference, or being different
freedom of expression	the right to say what you want in public
liberalism	political belief emphasising personal freedom
offensive	disgusting or insulting
pluralism	belief in a society in which people from different backgrounds and with different values should live together on an equal basis
political correctness	going to absurd lengths to avoid giving offence to certain groups in society
tolerance	accepting that other people have a right to do or say things that you may find offensive or may not agree with

■ BACKGROUND

This unit is about tolerance. At its root, tolerance is a willingness to accept that other people have the right to express views and practise forms of behaviour that you would not express or practise yourself, or may even think are wrong.

Why be tolerant and how tolerant should we be? First, tolerance can help to minimise social conflict and lead to a more cohesive and harmonious society. On this view, intolerance can only be justified where it relates to behaviour that seriously threatens the cohesion of society. Second, tolerance is a way of showing respect for people. This is an important democratic virtue in its own right. On this view, intolerance can only be justified where it relates to behaviour that fails to give people proper respect or denies their human rights. Third, tolerance is an essential element in liberalism. Liberal states operate on the principle of neutrality, i.e. the belief that no one set of moral or religious views, or way of life, should be promoted above another. On this view, intolerance can only be justified where it relates to behaviour that undermines the very principle of neutrality on which liberal belief is based – hence the expression: 'Tolerate everything except intolerance.'

There are two basic attitudes people can take towards tolerance. One is to agree to tolerate begrudgingly for pragmatic reasons. The other is to accept cheerfully other people's freedom to be different as a basic right that goes to the heart of what it is to live in a pluralistic democracy.

Precisely what things a pluralistic society ought or ought not to tolerate is a much more debateable question. These days, it is often discussed in the context of 'offensiveness' or 'giving offence'. Offensiveness is a complex concept. It has an emotional element to it, i.e. to find something offensive is to be hurt or upset by it. It may also involve a sense of being judged negatively by others. But it is largely a matter of perspective; what offends one person may not offend another because people's tastes and ability to cope with difference differ. The difficulty for law-makers is in determining the difference between dislikes that are just a matter of personal taste, and views and forms of behaviour that are, or ought to be outlawed as, *publicly* offensive.

The central activity in this unit revolves around a letter written to the head teacher of a school complaining about the behaviour of one of her teachers. The teacher in question has banned certain newspapers from the classroom on the grounds that they are offensive, only to find that in doing so his actions have given equal, if not more, offence to parents who read these papers on a daily basis.

This raises a number of questions about tolerance and the acceptance of diversity in society. Should we value all views and cultures equally or are there some things that society should just not tolerate? Does tolerance mean staying silent about things you disapprove of? Is giving offence to others in society something that can always and should always be avoided? If not, under what circumstances is it acceptable?

HOW TOLERANT SHOULD WE BE? Unit 8

▦ INTRODUCTION

This is a lesson about tolerance. In this lesson, you will learn what tolerance means, why people think it is important, and what things you think society in this country should and should not tolerate.

▦ STARTER

How tolerant are you?

Reflect upon these three questions:

- What are the most difficult things to put up with in a friend?
- Which of these do you think you should put up with even though it is difficult? Why?
- Where do you draw the line? Which of them would make you break friends with someone? Why?

> You can compare issues of tolerance in friendship with tolerance in society as a whole. The former relates to things we find difficult in a friend, yet we are prepared to put up with or accept they have a right to do; the latter to things we find difficult in other citizens, yet we are prepared to put up with or accept they have a right to do. The question in the former is: where should I draw the line? and in the latter: where should society draw the line?

▦ DEAR MRS PATTERSON

Read the letter of complaint from Mrs Ricci (Student Sheet 8.1, p65).

1. In pairs, improvise a conversation in which Mrs Ricci and the head teacher disagree about whether Mr Yardley was right to say what he did.

2. Share your work with the class.

3. In pairs, consider the following questions:

- What sort of arguments can Mrs Ricci use to uphold her complaint? How many different ones can you think of?

Suggested answers

- *the paper is freely available in any newsagents*
- *the paper is read by thousands of people*
- *it is not illegal*
- *the naked women are portrayed tastefully*
- *it is only a bit of fun*
- *Mr Yardley is just being arrogant: he thinks he can say what he likes because he thinks he is better than them*
- *it will make her daughter think she is not as good as the other students*
- *if the other students find out, they may pick on her daughter*
- *schools have no right to criticise how families live their lives.*

■ What sort of arguments can Mrs Patterson use to support Mr Yardley? How many different ones can you think of?

Suggested answers

- *students might find the paper offensive*
- *parents might find the paper offensive*
- *there would have been more complaints if Mr Yardley had not banned the paper*
- *this sort of paper degrades women/makes men think of them just as sex objects, not people/makes them value women only for their looks and their bodies, not their personalities or their abilities*
- *how would Mrs Ricci like it if it were pictures of her daughter?*
- *schools should stand up for the highest values in society, not the lowest ones*
- *imagine a class full of children giggling at pictures of naked women all lesson.*

You may wish to note down your thinking on Student Sheet 8.2, p66.

4. Share the arguments you have developed with the rest of the class.

■ Do you think Mrs Ricci had a right to complain? Why or why not?
■ Do you think Mr Yardley had a right to say what he did? Why or why not?

5. In small groups, study the topics on the Discussion Cards (Student Sheet 8.3, p67). Sort them into two groups:

■ things that you think should be TOLERATED in school
■ things that you think should not be TOLERATED in school.

Develop some arguments to support your decisions and then share them with the rest of the class.

■ PLENARY

Think of **one** thing that society in this country:

■ does not tolerate but which you think it should tolerate
■ does tolerate but which you think it should not tolerate.

Write down your ideas, with your reasoning, on two 'post-it' notes and stick them on the wall. Look at what other people in the class have written.

22 Tennyson Avenue
Stamford Green

11 April 2003

Dear Mrs Patterson,

I am writing to complain about one of your teachers.

Yesterday, Mr Yardley told the children in my daughter's English class that they all have to take a newspaper into the lesson next week. He said they could take any paper they liked, but it hadn't to be one of those 'offensive ones' with 'lots of naked women in'. Then he mentioned the name of a particular paper – I won't say which, but it is the one my family has been getting for years!

How dare he? It's not as though it's pornographic or anything. You can see it in any newsagents. Anyone can buy it – even a young child. It's not breaking the law. Thousands of people read it. There may be pictures of women in it, but so what? It's all done tastefully and only a bit of fun (something Mr Yardley doesn't seem to appreciate!).

Teachers have no right to tell children that the newspapers their parents read are offensive. If anybody is being offensive, it's Mr Yardley! Just because we haven't all been to some posh university like him! Doesn't he realise the message he is sending out to my daughter and the rest of her class – 'Those Riccis are no good, they read offensive papers'?

As the head teacher, it is your responsibility to do something about this. I would like to come and discuss this with you as soon as possible. Would you kindly arrange an appointment for me?

Yours sincerely,
Mrs D Ricci

☐ WHAT ARGUMENTS COULD THEY USE?

MRS RICCI	MRS PATTERSON

☐ DISCUSSION CARDS

Students putting up animal rights posters around school	**Students with body piercings**
Students opting out of RE lessons because they are not religious	**Students wearing T-shirts with the 'f' word on them on a non-uniform day**
Students writing letters to their local paper complaining about their teachers	**Religious groups 'preaching' in school or college assemblies**
Students kissing in the school corridor	**Students having time out of school for a religious festival**
Students setting up a school lesbian and gay support group	**Students expressing racist views in class discussions**

☐ RESEARCH TASK 1

■ TRADER GETS THE BOOT

A market trader was banned from selling shoes on the market in the seaside town of Morecambe for advertising steel toe-capped shoes as 'BNP boots'. Signs on his stall described the shoes as 'ex-British National Party jackboots worn in Burnley'.

The British National Party is a political party that has as one of its aims an all-white Britain. At the time, it had just been accused of involvement in race riots in the nearby town of Burnley.

Council officials visited the trader after a series of calls from local shops and concerned locals. A spokesman said: 'The offensive nature of the materials displayed left us with no alternative but to ban him.'

The trader said the signs were just a joke that had gone wrong.

1. What different arguments are there for and against banning the trader from selling the shoes? How many different ones can you think of?

2. What do you think of the council's decision? Why?

3. Do you think society should tolerate political parties that are openly racist? Should parties like that be made illegal? Explain the thinking behind your views.

4. Find out what the Commission for Racial Equality stands for and the main sorts of thing it does. You can find this at *www.cre.gov.uk*

☐ RESEARCH TASK 2

■ *BRITONS ARE 'GETTING MORE TOLERANT'*

As part of the nineteenth British Social Attitudes survey, more than 3,000 people were interviewed in 2002 on aspects of British life, including drugs, the family, race and sexuality prejudices, work, money habits, state spending, schools and transport.

The report showed that Britons are becoming less racist and less prejudiced against homosexuality with a more tolerant attitude towards cannabis.

It found that 54 per cent think cannabis should be legalised and 86 per cent believe doctors should be allowed to prescribe it. More than two thirds believed it should remain illegal when first asked 19 years ago.

47 per cent of Britons believe homosexuality is 'always' or 'mostly' wrong, compared with 70 per cent in 1985. A third now say it is 'not wrong at all'.

The number of people describing themselves as 'very' or 'a little' prejudiced against people from other races has dropped from 34 per cent in 1985 to 25 per cent.

The report's co-director Alison Park said, 'Some of the findings very much back up our common sense feeling of how people think, that they have become more liberal.'

1. How tolerant are people in your school, college or local neighbourhood? Carry out your own survey of people's attitudes towards the sort of controversial issues dealt with in the British Social Attitudes survey. If you prefer, survey what people think about other issues, e.g. asylum seekers, bad language on television, civil marriages for gay and lesbian couples. You will make the responses easier to record if you use questions that can be answered with a simple Yes/No/Don't know, or Agree/Disagree/Not sure. Remember to record the age and sex of each of the people you question.

2. Think of some way of sharing your findings with others in your school or college, students and teachers, e.g. a report, poster or video.

3. Find the most recent British Social Attitudes survey and write up its findings on one of the other issues it has investigated.

For information on British Social Attitudes surveys, go to *www.natcen.ac.uk*

■ AIMS

This unit aims to help students to:

■ become familiar with the idea of a free market

■ identify ways in which governments are able to regulate market forces

■ reflect upon the fairness of different trading practices.

■ CITIZENSHIP THEMES

■ How the economy functions

■ Rights and responsibilities of consumers, employers and employees

■ Legal and human rights and responsibilities

■ KEYWORDS

capitalism   economic system in which a country's trade and industry is controlled by private individuals and companies for profit rather than by the state

cartel   arrangement between two or more manufacturers or suppliers to keep prices high and restrict competition

command economy   economy highly regulated by central government

economy   how a country's finances are organised, including the production and supply of goods and services, wealth creation and employment

free market   system of buying and selling not regulated by government or outside authorities

laissez-faire   policy of not interfering in the workings of the market

market   place or process that brings buyers and sellers together

market forces   effects of unregulated buying and selling on trade

mixed economy   economy partly regulated by government and partly left to market forces

monopoly   where a manufacturer or supplier has a large enough share of the market to control or restrict the buying and selling of particular goods or services

predatory pricing   deliberately selling goods or services at loss in order to eliminate a competitor or competitors

price control   government setting the price at which goods or services are sold

price fixing   manufactures or suppliers of goods or services setting a common price at which all retailers are to sell them on to the consumer

■ BACKGROUND

This is a unit about market economics. The idea of market economics is that prices and wages should be allowed to fluctuate according to supply and demand rather than be subject to any form of outside control.

Supporters of market economics argue that the free market acts as an incentive to wealth creation, which is ultimately to the benefit of society as a whole. Some would go further and say that the market is a kind of 'natural' phenomenon and any form of outside interference in it is 'artificial' and therefore undesirable. Critics argue that an unregulated market tends to reinforce existing social inequalities, both in society and in the wider world. It can also have detrimental environmental consequences.

The practice in the UK has been to combine the development of a relatively free market with a high level of social welfare. In fact, for some, the main point of having a free market is to provide through private enterprise the resources needed to fund a decent level of social service provision. To this has been added a policy of trying to negate the worst effects of unregulated market forces by means of a combination of outlawing certain forms of trading practice as unfair and encouraging others through a range of government initiatives, i.e. a 'carrot-and-stick' approach. For example, on the one hand, UK law tries to prevent unfair competition between businesses by making it illegal to try to reduce competition by price fixing or predatory pricing. On the other hand, through the Common Agricultural Policy, it subsidises agricultural production and attempts to stimulate business in areas of high unemployment through assisted area grants.

The idea of the free market can also be extended to trade between, as well as within, states. Supporters of free trade argue for a system in which nations are able to trade with each other unimpeded by tariffs or other barriers. For example, free trade within its borders is one of the basics of the European Community. A free trade agreement between the US and Canada took effect in 1989 and was extended to Mexico in 1992 to complete the North American Free Trade Area (NAFTA). The problem with such agreements is that because the social and economic background of the partners involved is different, not everyone starts off on an equal footing, and that the advantages to partners may be to the disadvantage of countries outside the agreement.

The central activity in this unit involves an active learning game designed to simulate some of the key characteristics of life in a market economy. Students work in small groups to manufacture different paper shapes that they 'sell' to the teacher for 'money'. The distinctive aspect of the game, however, is that groups do not all start off with equal access to the basic resources, human and physical, required in the manufacturing process. This raises a number of questions. What are the advantages and disadvantages of a market economy? Should individuals and companies be allowed to trade completely free from outside interference or should they be subject to government control? How can fairer trading practices be encouraged?

Unit 9   IS FREE TRADE FAIR TRADE?

■ INTRODUCTION

This is a lesson about market forces. In this lesson, you will learn about the idea of a free market, about ways in which governments can interfere in the workings of the free market, and whether you think they are fair.

■ STARTER

Compare the prices of three video games in different shops. See Student Sheet 9.1, p75.

■ What explanation can you give for the difference in prices? How many different reasons can you think of?

Suggested answers
<ul><li>*higher/lower overheads*</li><li>*wish/need to make more/less profit per item*</li><li>*bought by the shop at a lower price*</li><li>*discounting to offload*</li><li>*selling cheap to build up customer loyalty*</li><li>*compensating by charging higher prices for other items*</li><li>*undercutting in the hope of selling more.*</li></ul>

■ Do you think shops should be allowed to charge whatever they like for the goods they sell? Why or why not?

■ MARKET FORCES

1. In small groups, play the 'Market Forces' game.

Your task is to imagine that you run a manufacturing company. The company manufactures paper shapes. The raw materials and the tools available for you to make your shapes will be found in the envelope on your desk.

Every completed shape you manufacture will earn a certain amount of money for your company – £70 for a circle, £30 for a square and £20 for a triangle.

When you have read the rules of the game (Student Sheet 9.2, p76) you can begin.

Preparation

Each group will need a large envelope containing some or all of the following equipment:

■ ruler
■ blank sheets of A4 paper
■ pencil
■ scissors
■ compasses.

The important thing is to vary the amount of equipment available to each group at the beginning of the game. In particular, you should ensure that there is at least:

■ one group with no scissors or compasses
■ one group with extra scissors and compasses
■ one group with no paper or ruler
■ one group with extra paper and an extra ruler.

Groups should also be given a copy of the rules and the template of the shapes they are to make with their prescribed measurements and exchange value (Student Sheet 9.3, p77).

You will need two volunteers to play the part of bankers. The job of the bankers is to measure shapes and pay for them. They will need to be strict and reject any shapes that fall short of the standard. The bankers also keep accounts of the number of shapes each group makes and their exchange value.

You will also need a volunteer to play the part of the supplier. The supplier sits with the bankers and looks after and sells spare blank paper.

Running the game

When the game has been under way for a while, you should begin to change some of the rules, for example, by saying:

■ 'Dealing with lots of small transactions is too time consuming, so from now on the bankers will only exchange shapes in bulk (specify number).'
■ 'Factories in the developing world are using cheap labour to produce shapes more cheaply than you and, as a result, the world price of shapes has gone down – circles are now £40, squares £20, and triangles £10.'
■ 'Due to a shortage of raw materials, the price of paper has now gone up to £150 a sheet.'
■ 'Supermarkets in this country who are main buyers of circles are selling circles off cheaply as loss-leaders – they are now only worth £20.'
■ 'The country where you export the bulk of your squares has introduced price controls making squares more expensive there. To remain competitive you have to reduce the selling price for squares to £10.'

End the game whenever you think fit and add up the money each group has made.

2. Share your experience of playing the game with the class.

■ Do you think the game was fair? Why or why not?

Suggested answers

FAIR:
- *the rules were the same for all*

UNFAIR:
- *each group had unequal amounts of equipment*
- *the prices kept changing*
- *people traded with each other unfairly.*

■ How did this make you feel? Did it alter your attitude towards other people in the class in any way? If so, how?
■ What, if anything, do you think could have been done to make the game fairer?

3. In small groups, think about trade in the real world. Do you think people should be completely free to trade exactly as they want or should there be rules they have to follow?

To help you think about this, look at the Discussion Cards (Student Sheet 9.4, pp78–79). The cards illustrate different ways in which governments can try to control the market.

Consider each one in turn and decide whether you think it is FAIR or UNFAIR to interfere in free trade in this way.

Think of some examples to support your decision. You may wish to note down your thinking on Student Sheet 9.5, p80.

4. Discuss your ideas with the class and see how far you are able to get class agreement on these issues.

■ *PLENARY*

Reflect upon the 'Market Forces' game. What sorts of thing do you think people can learn by playing this game? Write down two or three ideas and share them with the class.

★ □ COMPARING PRICES

Compare the prices of three video games in different shops:

PRODUCT	SHOP	PRICE
Halo	Play.com	£32.99
	CD-Wow	£32.99
	Swallow Games	£32.99
	MX2	£32.99
	Amazon UK	£34.99
	GamesPlanet	£34.99
	Software Products	£39.99
	W H Smith	£39.99

Halo 2	Play.com	£32.99
	CD-Wow	£32.99
	Swallow Games	£32.99
	Amazon UK	£29.99
	GamesPlanet	£36.99
	Game	£29.99

Halo: Combat Evolved	Gameloaded	£35.99
	Software Products	£37.99
	Game	£39.99

www.kelkoo.co.uk

☐ THE 'MARKET FORCES' GAME

Rules

The aim of the game is to make money by manufacturing paper shapes.

In order to do this, you have been provided with a number of items in an envelope and a template showing the sizes of the different shapes that are to be made.

You are free to trade any of these items with other groups if you wish – but under no circumstances should you use items other than the ones provided for the game.

Every completed shape you manufacture earns a certain amount of money for your group, but to guarantee payment, your shapes have to be cut to exactly the size shown in the template: smooth edges only, no shapes with jagged edges will be accepted.

Completed shapes should be taken to the bankers who will check your products for accuracy and, providing they are happy with what you have done, credit the money earned to your account.

Extra sheets of blank paper can be bought from the supplier at a cost of £100 a sheet.

Good luck!

★ □ TEMPLATE

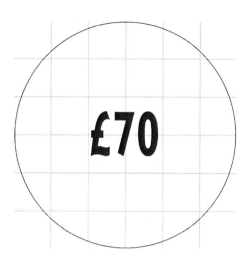

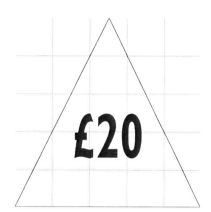

☐ DISCUSSION CARDS

A minimum wage

A government-set rate at which workers should be paid. For example, the minimum wage for 16–17 year-olds, 18–21 year-olds and over 21s in the UK.

Laws on working conditions

Government regulations affecting the conditions under which people work, such as health and safety, holidays, and working hours. For example, EU Working Time Regulations set a maximum working week of 48 hours, including overtime. You can agree to do more if you want, but under these rules your employer cannot pressurise you to do so.

Price controls

Government restrictions on the amount that private companies can charge for goods or services. For example, in 1999, the UK government put a cap on prices for electricity and water, knocking an average of five per cent off household bills for electricity and 14 per cent for water.

Advertising controls

Government rules about the way goods and services are promoted and advertised to the public. For example, the UK government's Advertising Standards Authority banned an advertising campaign for Rizla cigarette papers because it could be seen as condoning the use of cannabis.

Tariffs

Government tax on goods imported from abroad so people are more likely to buy ones produced at home. For example, in 2002, the US government imposed a tariff on imported steel of up to 30 per cent.

Subsidies

Government payments to cover part of the cost of goods or services, allowing them to be sold or supplied at a lower price. For example, EU subsidies to farmers guaranteeing them a higher price for their products.

Tax

Government tax affecting the sale or supply of certain goods or services. For example, value added tax (VAT).

Import quotas

Government-set limits on the amount of a product that can be imported into a country. For example, in 2003, the Russian government set up new annual meat import quotas on poultry, beef and pork.

Production quota

Government-set limits on the amount of a product an individual or a company can sell. For example, EU quotas on the amount of milk dairy farmers can sell.

Copyright laws

Government regulations making it illegal to sell cheap imitations of branded goods. For example, pirate CDs or videos.

Assisted area grants

Government grants to businesses located in certain areas. For example, regions with high unemployment.

Ethical codes

Government-set rules regulating the ethical behaviour of businesses. For example, about consumer rights, equal opportunities, pollution.

☆ INTERFERING IN THE MARKET

	Fair	Unfair	Depends	Reason
Minimum wage				
Price controls				
Tariffs				
Laws on working conditions				
Advertising controls				

	Fair	Unfair	Depends	Reason
Subsidies				
Tax				
Production quotas				
Assisted area grants				
Import quotas				
Copyright laws				
Ethical codes				

☐ RESEARCH TASK 1

■ *FOOTBALL KIT PRICE-FIXING CARTEL*

Some of the biggest names in sport were given fines totaling £18.6 million in August 2003 for artificially fixing the price of replica football strips. The penalties followed a two-year investigation by the Office of Fair Trading (OFT). The investigation found that agreements between the manufacturer Umbro and several leading clubs contravened the Competition Act, which came into force in 2000.

High street chain JJB Sports received the biggest fine, almost £8.4 million, followed by Umbro with £6.6 million, and Manchester United fined more than £1.6 million. The Football Association was also fined £158,000.

The shadow sport secretary, John Whittingdale, said: 'This shows that for too long the fans have been ripped off by a few of the top football clubs and businesses.'

In the course of its investigation, the OFT raided Umbro's HQ and seized documents that detailed a strategy to ensure stores sold their stock at pre-agreed prices. Any retailers refusing were to be struck off the supply list. Prices on the FA's online store were set at a level to match the price in branches of JJB Sports. The uniform price of £39.99 was reflected in nearly every high street outlet.

This sort of price fixing is illegal.

As soon as the fines were announced, prices for replica strips began to tumble. Stores were soon selling the strips at £25 – [that is,] £15 cheaper than they were before.

The Guardian, 2 August 2003

1. Find out more about the Office of Fair Trading. Write a short piece explaining some of the things it does.

2. Find out what is meant by a 'cartel'.

3. Carry out your own investigation into an area of trading where you think consumers are not getting value for money. Decide how you are going to present your findings and any recommendations you may wish to make.

For information about the Office of Fair Trading, go to *www.oft.gov.uk*

☐ RESEARCH TASK 2

■ *BRAZIL FIGHTS US FARM SUBSIDIES*

Cotton farmers in Brazil have complained to the World Trade Organisation that the US is destroying their industry.

The Brazilian farmers blame the collapse of their industry on subsidies paid out by the US government to American cotton growers.

Until the 1990s, cotton was Brazil's main export. However, when the price for cotton fell in the world market, many Brazilian farmers had no option but to stop growing it and move to other crops.

The US government gives billions of dollars in subsidies to American cotton farmers. The subsidies mean farmers receive a guaranteed price for their cotton, no matter what the world price. With these subsidies, American farmers have produced even more cotton – pushing the world market price down even further.

Oxfam estimates that the US government spends three times more on its cotton farmers than the American aid budget for all of Africa's 500 million people.

It says: 'This makes a mockery of the idea of a level playing field. The rules are rigged against the poor.'

The Guardian, 28 September 2002

1. Why might the US government want to spend so much money in subsidies for cotton farmers? How many different reasons can you think of?

2. Do you think the subsidies to the US cotton farmers are fair? What different arguments are there for and against this?

3. Find out about work of:
   - ■ World Trade Organisation
   - ■ Oxfam
   - ■ Fair Trade Foundation.

Write a short piece comparing the different ways in which each of these organisations tries to make trade fairer.

4. Carry out your own research into an area of trade in which producers are subsidised by a government. Reflect upon the fairness of the subsidies you have researched. Decide how to present the information you have discovered and your feelings about it.

For information about the World Trade Organisation, go to *www.wto.org*
For Oxfam, go to *www.maketradefair.com* and *www.oxfam.org.uk*
For the Fair Trade Organisation, go to *www.fairtrade.org.uk*

Government

▣ AIMS

This unit aims to help students to:

- understand why people have governments

- become familiar with a range of things governments can be responsible for

- reflect upon the sorts of personal obligation that governments often demand of their citizens

- learn about the different functions of the system of government in the UK.

▣ CITIZENSHIP THEMES

- Central and local government

- Parliamentary and other forms of government

- Public services and how they are financed

▣ KEYWORDS

common good	for the good of the community as a whole
community	group of people joined together for a common purpose
government	(1) system by which a state is ruled (2) body of people responsible for ruling a state
parliament	body of people with the power to make and change laws
politics	to do with how a community is ruled and who has the authority, power and influence to decide this
private	non-public, to do with people as individuals, members of families, or friendship or voluntary groups
public	to do with the state, the community as a whole, or people in general
state	an area or community with its own government
the State	body of people within a state responsible for all aspects of rule within that state – it is larger than government, and includes the courts, the police and the army

▣ BACKGROUND

This unit is about the concept of government. With the exception of certain small-scale nomadic groups, almost all societies have some form of government. Government is the system by which a society is ruled. A system of community-wide rule means people living and working together, not out of friendship or ties of blood, but in order to achieve goals that are in the interests of the community as a whole and that are not achievable by individual effort. As a rule, the benefits of some kind of formal system of collective decision-making are seen as outweighing the personal sacrifices that need to be made to make the system work.

There is more to running a country than making and changing rules, however. Rules have to be enforced and conflicts about rules need to be arbitrated – hence the need for some form of policing and for courts of law. Taken together, institutions of this kind are often referred to as 'the State'. The State, therefore, includes, but is much more than, government. It comprises all the institutions that are concerned with aspects of formal rule in a society.

Granted that some form of state is necessary, what are its essential functions? This is more controversial. Some people take the narrow view that the function of the state should be restricted to protecting the safety of its citizens and providing some forms of legal justice. Others have a much wider concept and maintain that the duty of the state extends to responsibility for social welfare, employment, education, health care, the economy, environmental protection and the provision of social justice.

Young people can find the relationship between the concepts of 'government' and 'state' difficult. For many they are synonymous. To all extents and purposes, therefore, this unit starts out by treating the two concepts as though they were the same – asking about the functions of the government when technically it is the functions of the State that is meant. It is up to teachers to make the distinction clear.

The central activity in the unit is a story about a tribe of nomadic people who wander the rainforest in isolated family units and thus have no real form of government. As the rainforest begins to shrink under the pressure from outside force, however, it becomes clear that the only way for the Arinoco to preserve their way of life will be for individual family groups to put aside their differences and work together as a community with their own government. The problem is that none of the tribe has ever thought about acting in this way before.

This raises important questions. Why do we need a State? What are the essential functions of the State? What sort of personal sacrifices are worth making for the sake of society as a whole?

Answer to question 2, Three Levels of Government, p91: 21 for each

Unit 10 WHY DO WE NEED A GOVERNMENT?

■ INTRODUCTION

This lesson is about government. In this lesson, you will learn why people have governments, about the different sorts of things that governments can do, and about the sorts of things that the UK government does do.

■ STARTER

In small groups, look at the topics on the Discussion Cards (Student Sheet 10.1, p88). Sort them into issues in which you think the government in this country is:

■ INVOLVED
■ NOT INVOLVED.

> All the topics are currently the concern of the UK government in one way or another – even if it is only in the form of laws designed to protect neighbours from overloud music.
>
> The activity raises the question of what governments are for. The exercise that follows tries to explore this question by focusing on a group of people that do not have any form of government – at least not in the sense of having anything approaching the apparatus of a State.

■ IS TIME RUNNING OUT FOR THE ARINOCO?

Read the article about the Arinoco (Student Sheet 10.2, p89).

1. As a class, discuss briefly the main things you think the tribe would stand to gain or to lose if it were to become a single community with its own government. You may wish to note down your thinking on Student Sheet 10.3, p90.

Suggested answers

GAIN:
- *easier to defend themselves from hostile tribes*
- *better able to prevent squabbles between families*
- *able to share out food more fairly*
- *able to ensure access to clean water for all*
- *able to look after the sick/prevent disease better*
- *better placed to make a stand against the people chopping down the trees.*

LOSE:
- *some of their customs and ways of worshipping the spirits of the forest*
- *power to make all their own decisions*
- *their individuality*
- *personal freedoms, including freedom of movement*
- *traditional ways of growing crops and hunting*
- *may have to give up water, food, fuel, etc., to share with others.*

2. In pairs, improvise a dialogue between two Arinoco people. One of you thinks all the families should get together and work as a single community, and the other thinks you will be better off staying as you are.

3. As a class, reflect upon the dialogues you have improvised. Then consider these questions:

■ What sort of issues do you think the tribe would be better deciding as a community? Why?

Suggested answers

- *defending themselves from enemy tribes*
- *food*
- *water*
- *health care/prevention of disease*

- *fuel*
- *inter-family squabbles*
- *what to do about the people chopping down the trees.*

■ What sort of issues do you think it would be all right to decide in the old way – by each family? Why?

Suggested answers

- *behaviour within the family*
- *clothing*

- *how they worship the spirits of the forest.*

4. In small groups, think about the different arrangements the Arinoco will need to put in place in order to have their own system of government. Draw up a list of the kind of questions they will need to think about, e.g.,

■ Who will make the rules?
■ How will the person or persons that makes the rules be chosen?
■ What should happen to people who do not keep the rules?

You may wish to develop this exercise into a separate lesson in which groups are given the task of creating a system of government appropriate to the needs of the people they are discussing – establishing the kind of institutions they will need, their roles, how they will be funded and organised, e.g. a parliament, police force, military, courts, etc.

5. Share your questions with the rest of the class. Which ones do you think will be the most difficult to decide? Why?

PLENARY

On your own, write down what you think is the most important thing a government should be responsible for and why. Go round the class and compare your views.

☐ DISCUSSION CARDS

Crime	**Drugs**
Music	**Holidays**
Sport	**Education**
Pets	**Money**
War	**Exams**
Food	**Environment**

☐ IS TIME RUNNING OUT FOR THE ARINOCO?

A report on a way of life that is rapidly disappearing.

The Arinoco is a tribe of people that lives deep in the rainforest. They have no settled homes and wander from place to place in small family units.

Every Arinoco family is a law unto itself. It grows its own crops, does its own hunting, and builds its own shelters. It makes its own decisions and sorts out its own problems – with the oldest man in the family usually having the final say. It has its own customs and ways of worshipping the spirits of the rainforest.

The one thing that all the tribe has in common is its language. Not that everyone speaks exactly the same. Arinoco families in the mangrove swamps, for example, have great difficulty understanding Arinoco families in the mountains, and vice versa.

This was not a problem in the old days. The rainforest was huge. Arinoco families never saw each other except to pick a wife or husband. There was enough land for everyone. There was an endless supply of fuel and plenty of fresh water to drink. Enemy tribes kept their distance and everyone was able to live in peace.

However, all this changed when the rainforest began to shrink. People from outside have chopped down many of the trees to grow grass for their cattle. The Arinoco families, about 200 in all, have been pushed together into a smaller and smaller area. Food is scarce, water supplies are contaminated and disease is spreading. Fights are breaking out between different families, and clashes with other tribes are becoming more common.

It is clear to everyone outside the rainforest – but not yet to the Arinoco themselves – that if their way of life is to survive, the separate families will have to put aside their differences and work together as a single community with their own form of government.

The problem is that they have never had any form of government before.

What could we say to persuade them that it might be a good idea?

□ SHOULD THE ARINOCO HAVE A GOVERNMENT?

LOSE	GAIN

☐ RESEARCH TASK 1

■ *THREE LEVELS OF GOVERNMENT*

For British citizens, there are three levels, or 'tiers', of government.

Local councils They make decisions that govern life in the local community. There are different kinds depending upon where you live, e.g. district, borough and county councils.

British Parliament This meets at Westminster in London and makes decisions that govern life throughout Britain.

European Parliament This meets at Brussels in Belgium and Strasbourg in France. It makes decisions that govern life in all the countries in the European Union, including Britain.

In addition, Scotland has its own parliament in Edinburgh; Wales has its National Assembly in Cardiff, and Northern Ireland has its Assembly in Belfast.

The European Parliament in session, Strasbourg.

1. What sort of decisions is each of these levels of government responsible for? Find some examples for each.

2. How old does a person have to be before they can stand as a candidate in an election for:
   - a local council
   - the British Parliament
   - the European Parliament?

3. Which countries belong to the European Union? Draw a map showing where they are.

4. What is 'devolution'?

For information on government and politics, go to *www.youthinformation.com*

★ □ RESEARCH TASK 2

■ *SMACKING: WHO SHOULD DECIDE?*

Is it all right to smack children if they have been naughty? At the moment, the law in England and Wales allows parents to use 'reasonable chastisement' on their children.

However, some people think this law should be changed. They want the government to ban parents from smacking their children altogether. Others disagree. They say that it is not up to the government to decide this kind of thing; it is up to the parents.

This raises the questions, what sort of decisions is it right for the government to make, and what sort of decisions are best left to citizens and their families?

1. What are the arguments for and against allowing parents to smack their children? How many different ones can you find?

2. Do you think this should be up to the government to decide, or is it a decision best left to parents? Why?

3. What do people mean when they talk about a 'nanny state'?

For information about the debate on smacking, go to *www.learn.co.uk/ glearning/secondary/topical/ks3/ smacking*

WHAT IS THE BEST WAY TO RUN A COUNTRY?

■ AIMS

This unit aims to help students to:

- become familiar with different types of political system

- understand some of the strengths and weaknesses of different types of political system

- learn about the type of political system in the UK.

■ CITIZENSHIP THEMES

- Parliamentary and other forms of government

- The electoral system and the importance of voting

■ KEYWORDS

democracy — system of government in which power lies with the people as a whole or their representatives

dictatorship — system of government in which a single person or political party rules with almost unlimited power

government — (1) way in which a country is run
(2) body of people that runs a country

monarchy — system of government in which power lies with a king or queen, or royal family

parliament — body of people with the power to make and change laws

republic — country with an elected president or head of state

sovereignty — supreme political authority in a country

theocracy — system of government in which power lies with priests or religious leaders

■ BACKGROUND

This unit is about different political systems, or forms of government. Political systems are usually classified in terms of:

- who holds political power, for example, a single person, a particular group or party, or the people as a whole

- how political power is conferred on people, for example, through birth, membership of a particular party or faction, or by right of citizenship

- how rule is enforced, for example, by force or consent.

The principal ones are democracy, monarchy, theocracy and tyranny (now usually known as a 'dictatorship').

Political systems can also be distinguished in terms of where sovereignty lies in a state. Sovereignty means supreme authority. Within a theocracy, for example, sovereignty is thought to lie with God and is mediated through God's representative(s) on Earth. Within a democracy, sovereignty may be thought to lie in a definite institution, such as Parliament, or in a more abstract concept such as the 'will of the people'. Within a monarchy, sovereignty lies in a royal family – perhaps ultimately in God if the royal family is believed to rule by 'divine right'. Within a dictatorship, it lies in the dictator or ruling party.

Systems such as these are 'ideal types', of course. In reality, they can co-exist in the same country. For example, a parliamentary democracy may contain elements of dictatorship within it or co-exist with a ruling royal family or national religion. This allows us to ask questions such as how democratic is our country?

So what is the *best* way of running a country? Each system has its strengths and weaknesses. For example, a dictatorship may provide strong leadership and national unity, but it will not necessarily be responsive to the wishes of its citizens or guarantee them human rights. A democracy, on the other hand, may be more responsive to the wishes and rights of its citizens, but may be less effective at times of national crisis.

One way of assessing the comparative strengths and weaknesses of different types of system is to ask how much each contributes to important social ideals, such as national unity, peace, economic prosperity, social justice, individual liberties and freedoms, equality, tolerance, welfare, law and order, and human rights.

The central activity in this unit is a role-play in which students take the parts of delegates at a national conference called to determine the form of government best suited to their country. Tashbekistan is an imaginary country, struggling to find its feet after 20 years of war. Delegates at the national conference have to choose between bringing back their former king from exile, handing over power to the priests, introducing some form of parliamentary democracy, or continuing with the relatively benign dictatorship of the Tashbek warlord who, though ruthless, has been responsible for driving out the enemy from their country.

This raises important questions. Is there an ideal form of government, one that is always best regardless of the situation? Or are different types of political system suited to different circumstances?

Research task, What Form of Government? p101. Answers:

- Spain – democracy, constitutional monarchy

- Cuba – communist dictatorship

- Iran – theocracy, Islamic republic

- Ireland – democracy, republic

- USA – democracy, republic

- Germany – democracy, federal republic

- The Netherlands – democracy, constitutional monarchy

- Australia – democracy, constitutional monarchy

- Swaziland – monarchy

WHAT IS THE BEST WAY TO RUN A COUNTRY?

■ INTRODUCTION

This is a lesson about different forms of government. In this lesson, you will learn about different ways of running a country, about some of their strengths and weaknesses, and about the way in which the UK is run.

■ STARTER

Who do you think runs this country? Is it:

■ the Queen
■ the Prime Minister
■ Parliament
■ you?

Discuss your answers briefly as a class.

The answer? All are true in part – under-18s are represented by MPs, too! This is an opportunity for a two-minute explanation of the system of government in the UK as it stands at the moment. It raises the question, is this the best way to run a country? This naturally leads into a consideration of what the alternatives are.

■ THE GRAND ASSEMBLY

Read the information about **The Grand Assembly** (Student Sheet 11.1, p97).

1. In small groups, imagine you are delegates at the Grand Assembly and that tomorrow you will have a chance to decide how your country should be run. Think about the situation your country is in at the moment. What would you want a new government to do first?

   You will find some suggestions on the Discussion Cards (Student Sheet 11.2, p98). Put these suggestions in order, 1–9, in terms of importance as you see them. Think of some reasons to support your decision.

2. Come out of role and share your thinking with the class. Are governments really able to order their priorities in this way or do you think they would do it differently in reality?

Suggested answers

YES:
- *a government will want to do what it thinks is most important first*

NO:
- *a government usually has to deal with a number of different priorities at the same time – it is just that it gives them different emphasis.*

3. Divide into four groups and return to role. Choose one of the Role-Play Cards (Student Sheet 11.3, p99) for your group. Each group should take a different role. Each card contains a different way of running the country. Your task as a group is to argue as strongly as you can for your given option.

   In your groups, develop some arguments to support the view on your card. Try to predict the sort of arguments that other groups might use to support their options and prepare some counter-arguments. Decide what each of your group members is going to say in the Grand Assembly.

4. Join together with all the other groups for the Grand Assembly. In role, tell the others what your choice of government is and why you think it is the best way forward for your country. Challenge the other groups on any points you disagree with.

> You may wish to rearrange the room so that the supporters of each view sit around four sides of a square.

5. Come out of role and think about all the arguments you have heard. What do you think are the advantages and disadvantages of each of the four different ways of running a country you have discussed? You may wish to note down your thinking on Student Sheet 11.4, p100.

> You may wish to write the names of the four political systems on each of the four sides of the room. Put up two large pieces of paper on each labelled 'Advantages' and 'Disadvantages'. Then give the class five minutes to go round and write up their ideas or provide them with 'post-it' notes to attach to the wall. The class may then go round again to see what everyone has written or volunteers can read it out.

6. Take a class vote on what you think is the best way of running a country like Tashbekistan.

PLENARY

On your own, reflect upon the way that the UK is run. What form of government would you say is in place in this country? Why do you think this? Write down your answer. Go round the class and compare your answers.

☐ THE GRAND ASSEMBLY

Tashbekistan is a poor country, consisting largely of steep mountain ranges and windswept plains. The people who live there are divided into a number of different ethnic groups. They all follow the same religion, but each has its own language and customs – a fact that has often led to suspicion and sometimes violence between them.

Twenty years ago, large reserves of natural gas and oil were discovered in Tashbekistan. Shortly afterwards, the country was invaded by one of its neighbours. The king fled into exile and the country entered a period of almost permanent war and fighting.

The invaders were finally driven out six months ago, but the people still live in fear. Schools and hospitals have been destroyed; crops have been pulled up; there is not enough food to go round; crime has become a way of life and guns are carried openly in the streets.

Tomorrow is the day of the Grand Assembly. More than 1,500 delegates from the different ethnic groups are meeting to decide how the country should be run now it is no longer at war.

The man in charge of the country at the moment is a Tashbek warlord called Za. Za is a strong man who will stop at nothing to get his way. During the war, he was able to unite the majority of the different ethnic groups behind him to fight back against the invaders, although a minority sided with the enemy in the hope of being better off if their country was eventually taken over from outside.

Then there is the king. His family ruled the country single-handedly for several generations. Now the war is over, the king is keen to return to his royal palace and serve his people once again.

Before the royal family came to power, the country used to be run by the priests. These men (no women can be priests) live simple lives of study and prayer, sharing their food with the poor and needy. The priests have a growing following in the country districts where many people feel that it is lack of respect for religion that has got the country into the state it is in today.

Finally, there are people – a much smaller group, mainly in the towns – who take a different view altogether. They want the country to be run by a parliament with elections in which all people have a vote.

The decision facing the Grand Assembly will be a difficult one. What do you think it should decide?

☐ DISCUSSION CARDS

Punish the people who supported the invaders

Defend your country against further attacks from outside

Rebuild your schools and hospitals

Bring equality for women

Bring law and order to the streets

Provide food for starving people

Develop the oil wells and gas supplies

Unite all the different ethnic groups

Plant crops for next year

☐ ROLE-PLAY CARDS

A

You want the warlord, Za, to continue running the country as he was doing during the war.

B

You want the priests to take over running the country again as they once used to.

C

You want the king to come back and take over running the country as he was doing before he went into exile.

D

You want the country to be run by a parliament of men and women chosen in an election in which every citizen has a vote.

☐ ADVANTAGES AND DISADVANTAGES

Monarchy

Advantage:

_____

_____

_____

_____

Disadvantage:

_____

_____

_____

_____

Democracy

Advantage:

_____

_____

_____

_____

Disadvantage:

_____

_____

_____

_____

Theocracy

Advantage:

_____

_____

_____

Disadvantage:

_____

_____

_____

_____

Dictatorship

Advantage:

_____

_____

_____

_____

Disadvantage:

_____

_____

_____

_____

☐ RESEARCH TASKS

■ CONSTITUTIONAL MONARCHY

The Queen at the State Opening of Parliament.

The government in the UK at the moment is a 'constitutional monarchy'. This means that although the Queen is technically the Head of State, it is Parliament that makes and changes laws. In theory, the Queen can still reject bills that Parliament passes and prevent them from becoming laws, but the last time a monarch did this was in 1702.

1. Make a collection of newspaper articles that feature the Queen or the royal family. What do these tell you about the role of the monarchy in Britain in the twenty-first century and people's attitudes towards it?

2. On the whole, do you think the UK benefits from having a royal family? Write a short statement setting out the arguments for and against, and which you think are the stronger.

■ WHAT FORM OF GOVERNMENT?

What system of government is in place in each of the following countries?

- Spain
- Cuba
- Iran
- Ireland
- USA
- Germany
- The Netherlands
- Australia
- Swaziland

Unit 12 — HOW CAN EVERYONE HAVE AN EQUAL SAY?

■ AIMS

This unit aims to help students to:

■ become familiar with different ideas of democracy

■ learn about different voting systems

■ reflect upon the advantages and disadvantages of different voting systems.

■ CITIZENSHIP THEMES

■ The electoral system and the importance of voting

■ Parliamentary and other forms of government

■ Legal and human rights and responsibilities

■ KEYWORDS

constituency	(1) section of the population from which a politician or political party draws support (2) geographical area whose inhabitants elect a representative to Parliament
constitution	set of rules, written or unwritten, that governs the way an organisation is run
delegate	representative who is under instruction to act or vote in a particular way
democracy	system of government in which power lies with the people or their representatives
direct democracy	system of government in which decisions are taken directly by the people
electorate	people entitled to vote in elections
parliament	body of people with the power to make and change laws
political party	group of people with a particular set of political beliefs, formed to elect people to Parliament
referendum	vote taken by the people to decide a particular political issue rather than to elect representatives to Parliament
representative	person chosen to act or vote on behalf of a community or number of people
representative democracy	system of government in which decisions are taken by elected representatives on behalf of the people as a whole

■ BACKGROUND

This unit is about democracy. Democracy is first and foremost about political equality. It is about everyone involved in a community having an equal say in the running of that community. In practice, this means two different things:

■ majority voting

■ free and open debate.

Although most people believe in democracy as the ideal form of government, there is considerable disagreement about how it should be put into practice. 'Direct' democracy – a system in which all citizens vote directly on an issue – may have the advantage of being immediate and be a good way of reflecting grassroots opinion, but it is very time consuming and can stretch the technical knowledge and understanding of the ordinary voter. For these reasons, modern societies usually reserve forms of direct democracy for issues affecting the basic constitution of a country, e.g. entry into the European Union, devolved parliaments for the regions.

'Representative' democracy – a system in which citizens elect fellow citizens to act and make decisions on their behalf – is not without its problems, however. One problem relates to the role of the representative. Are representatives meant to:

■ stand up for the views of the citizens who voted for them, or

■ reflect the feelings of the electorate as a whole, or

■ pursue their own ideals?

A second problem relates to the manner in which they are to be elected. Should representatives be elected:

■ as individuals or as members of a political party?

■ by the first-past-the-post system or some form of proportional representation?

Thirdly, should the make-up of an elected parliament be representative of the general make-up of society, e.g. in ethnic, gender or age terms? If so, how is this to be achieved?

Perhaps one of the most intractable problems is finding a form of democracy that prevents dominant groups in society from ignoring the interests and views of minority groups – what is sometimes called the 'tyranny of the majority'. This is one of the reasons for having a formal constitution.

The central activity in this unit revolves around an allegorical story in which a group of farm animals consider the consequences of making decision-making on their farm more democratic. The story raises a number of questions about democracy as a way of organising community life e.g.,

- What is the most effective form of democracy?

- In a democracy, how can you ensure that minority groups are listened to and not outvoted all the time?

- At what age should someone be entitled to vote?

- Does participation in a democratic society require special skills or knowledge? If so, how are they to be gained?

- What should society do about people who refuse to participate or use their vote?

- What is fairest way of electing representatives?

- Whose views is an elected representative meant to represent?

Unit 12 HOW CAN EVERYONE HAVE AN EQUAL SAY?

■ INTRODUCTION

This is a lesson about democracy. In this lesson, you will learn about different ideas of democracy, different types of voting systems in use in the UK, and what you think are their advantages and disadvantages.

■ STARTER

How can you explain it?

- In the 1951 general election, the Labour Party got 49 per cent of the votes and lost to the Conservatives. Yet in the 1997 general election, it got only 44 per cent of the votes and beat the Conservatives with a massive majority.
- In the 1997 general election, the Liberal Democrats got 700,000 less votes than in 1992, yet gained an extra 26 MPs in Parliament.

How can you explain these results? What different reasons can you think of?

Suggested answers

- *caused by having more than two parties in the running – depends upon the proportion of votes the other parties got*
- *number of MPs is not proportionate to number of votes in the first-past-the-post system*

■ ANIMAL PARLIAMENT

To help you think about the fairness of voting systems, read **Animal Parliament** (Student Sheet 12.1, pp106–107).

1. In pairs, think about the arguments for and against the animals deciding things for themselves. How many different ones can you find? You may wish to note down your thinking on Student Sheet 12.2, p108.

Suggested answers

FOR:

- *it is not fair that one animal should dictate how the others live*
- *it gives animals a chance to express/share their points of view*
- *the animals have a right to a say in the things that affect them.*

AGAINST:

- *there would be chaos if all of them were involved*
- *everyone knows where they stand at the moment*
- *some animals are too ignorant to know what to do with a vote*
- *it is time consuming and impractical*
- *it will be unfair on the pigs*
- *big groups of animals will always be able to outvote smaller ones*
- *it is difficult to known which animals should/should not be allowed to vote*
- *the group may vote for something that conflicts with individual conscience.*

2. Imagine the animals decide to elect their own parliament. In small groups, look at the suggestions on the Discussion Cards (Student Sheet 12.3, p109). Decide what you think are the advantages and disadvantages of each of these different voting systems. Which do you think is the best? Why? You may wish to note down your thinking on Student Sheet 12.4, p110.

3. Present your ideas to the class for discussion.

4. In your small groups, draw up a set of rules, no more than five or six, to help make sure the animal parliament is run fairly. Issues to think about include:

- the balance between representatives of different species
- the balance between male and female representatives
- how to prevent the parliament being used by some animals to discriminate against others
- the animals that should or should not be entitled to vote
- whether voting should be compulsory
- which issues should be decided by the parliament and which by a vote involving all the animals eligible to vote.

5. Share your work with the class. Is it possible to agree a class decision on this?

6. As a class, think about the role of the animal representatives. Once they are elected, do you think the animal representatives should be able to act and vote as they like? Should they only be allowed to act and vote as instructed by the animals that voted for them? What do you think? Why?

■ *PLENARY*

Reflect upon what you have learned from this lesson. What do you think are the most important things the animal parliament exercise can teach people about politics in real life? Write down three or four ideas and share them with the class.

☐ ANIMAL PARLIAMENT

One day, Farmer Giles rose early and drove off to the agricultural show with Rex, his loyal sheepdog.

When the farmer and his dog were safely out of sight, some of the farm animals gathered together in the big barn.

'Phewww!' said Emily the sheep. 'I'm sick to death of being bossed around by that sheepdog!'

'Me, too,' said Francis, the fat, furry farm cat. 'It's not fair that one farm animal should be able to tell all the others what to do.'

'Yes. Farm animals should be able to make their own decisions,' said Emily.

'No way!' grunted Sid the pig. 'There'd be chaos if you let farm animals make their own decisions. At least you know where you stand with Rex.'

'But think how much fairer it would be if we *all* had a say in things,' said Emily. 'One animal, one vote.'

'What's so fair about one animal, one vote?' grunted Sid. 'I'll tell you the first thing that'd happen. You'd all gang up against the pigs and vote for a ban on mud – or at least to reduce it to such an extent that it's not worth wallowing in. We pigs are always getting little digs about our mud-wallowing habits and how "offensive" they are.'

'Oooooh!' said Emily. 'We'd never take a vote on anything without discussing it first. Pigs should get the same chance to explain their point of view as the next farm animal.'

'And *then* get outvoted!' grunted Sid.

'Don't be so negative,' said Emily. 'Have more faith in your fellow farm animals.'

☐ ANIMAL PARLIAMENT

'Fellow farm animals?' said Sid. 'What counts as a "fellow farm animal", for mud's sake? Does it include bees, for example? One animal, one vote and the bees would get their own way every time. There's thousands of the little buzzers in the orchard.'

'And don't even *think* about giving ducks a vote,' said Damian, the insensitive chicken. 'Ducks wouldn't have a clue what to do with a vote if they got one – not a cluckin' clue.'

'Ducks have as much right to a say in things that affect them as other farm animals,' replied Gordon, the rather more sensitive donkey. 'What worries *me* is what would happen if you all voted for something beastly that went against my conscience – like taking revenge on Rex. You know how I feel about violence.'

'We all respect your views, Gordon,' said Emily, 'but you can't go against a vote just because you don't like it.'

'I'd vote for taking revenge on Rex, no problem,' whispered Francis, the fat, furry farm cat.

'I've…been…thinking,' mooed Mollie the lugubrious cow. 'Voting is not a bad idea…and discussing is not a bad idea…either…But if we all had to discuss *everything*…nothing would ever get decided.'

'And if we all had to vote on *every* decision, nothing would ever get done,' interrupted Francis.

'What we should do,' suggested Mollie, 'is elect a small group of farm animals to do some of the discussing and voting…for us.'

'An animal parliament!' the animals chorused in unison.

'What's the betting it's never a pig that gets elected?' grunted Sid.

To be continued…

☐ SHOULD THE ANIMALS DECIDE FOR THEMSELVES?

FOR	AGAINST

☐ DISCUSSION CARDS

A

Animals of each species elect one of their members to represent the species, e.g. cows elect a cow, sheep elect a sheep, and so on.

B

Different species are grouped together in terms of things they have in common, e.g. size, diet, and so on. Each group elects one of its members to represent the group.

C

The farm is divided into different areas. Animals in each area elect one of the animals that lives there to represent the area.

D

Animals elect a set number of fellow animals to represent the farm as a whole.

☆ ☐ ADVANTAGES AND DISADVANTAGES

■ *VOTING SYSTEMS*

	Advantage	Disadvantage
A		
B		
C		
D		

☐ RESEARCH TASK 1

■ *PROPORTIONAL REPRESENTATION*

MPs elected to the UK Parliament are chosen by a system called 'first-past-the-post'. Under this system, the country is divided up into different areas, called constituencies, each of which selects its own MP. All the voters in a constituency have one vote and the winning candidate is the one with the most votes – even though the majority of people may not have voted for that person.

Some people believe that this system is unfair and argue that MPs should be chosen by some form of 'proportional representation'. Proportional representation is a way of trying to make sure that every vote cast contributes to the overall position of the party voted for.

1. There are a number of different systems of proportional representation. Find out how the following systems work:
   - list system
   - additional member system
   - single transferable vote system.

2. Find out which system of proportional representation is used for elections to:
   - the Scottish Parliament
   - the Welsh Assembly
   - the European Parliament.

3. What are the main arguments for and against proportional representation? Which do you think is fairer – proportional representation or the first-past-the-post system? Why?

For information about different voting systems, go to
www.electoral-reform.org.uk

☐ RESEARCH TASK 2

■ *SUMMERHILL SCHOOL*

At Summerhill School, decisions are made at the weekly meeting. At the meeting, anyone can raise a subject for discussion or propose a motion to vote on and everyone has one vote – from members of staff to the youngest of the pupils.

All changes to the school rules are made at the meeting. Accusations of people having broken the rules are dealt with at another meeting of the whole school, called the tribunal, which also takes place weekly.

Up to 70 people of different ages attend the meeting. The chairperson is usually one of the older pupils. He or she can fine anyone for making a noise, ask them to sit elsewhere, or throw them out altogether. Not only do pupils have equal power in the meeting, they also greatly outnumber the adults.

Recent school rules include:
- you must have working front and back brakes on your bike
- you cannot ride little kids' bikes – even with permission
- you cannot watch TV during lessons or meal times
- no graffiti (penalty: £1 fine), except on the special graffiti wall where graffiti is allowed.

There are certain things the meeting is not allowed to decide, e.g. teachers' pay, hiring and firing of staff, building work. The principle is that pupils should have the power to make decisions over what is important in their daily lives. Bringing these other subjects to the meeting would burden them with unnecessary worries rather than increase their freedom.

1. Compare the advantages and disadvantages of this form of decision-making with having an elected school or college council. Which do you think is the better system? Why?

2. In what ways is the system of decision-making at Summerhill School similar to, and different from, the one in place in your school or college? Do you think it is any fairer? Why or why not?

3. Conduct your own survey into whether young people feel they have enough power to make decisions over what is important in their daily lives at your school or college. You may wish to compare their views with those of the adult staff. Decide how you are going to present your findings and any recommendations you wish to make.

■ AIMS

This unit aims to help students to:

■ become familiar with different kinds of welfare benefits

■ learn how they are organised and paid for

■ consider how fair it is to expect the state to be responsible for these.

■ CITIZENSHIP THEMES

■ Public services and how they are financed

■ The work of voluntary groups

■ KEYWORDS

culture of dependency	when people come to rely upon state welfare so much that they have difficulty taking responsibility for their own lives
means test	check made on a person's wealth to see whether they qualify for a welfare benefit
National Insurance	system of tax in which weekly payments from employers and employees are used to provide welfare benefits for the population as a whole
private sector	jobs and services provided by private individuals and companies rather than the state
public sector	jobs and services provided by the state through central and local government
universal benefit	benefit available to all regardless of their wealth
voluntary sector	jobs and services provided by groups of people organised on a charitable, 'self-help' basis
welfare	(1) well-being (2) money or services provided by the state to help citizens at times of need, e.g. illness, unemployment
welfare state	system of social security and services provision in which the state takes chief responsibility for the welfare of citizens

■ BACKGROUND

This is a unit about social welfare. Traditionally, the idea of the welfare state was to support citizens during vulnerable periods in their lives, e.g. ill health, retirement, pregnancy, unemployment. A key point in the development of this idea was the National Insurance Act, 1911. This formalised the notion that all people should pay into a central fund that could be accessed by individuals in time of need. It was incorporated into UK law in 1945, largely following the blueprint of the Beveridge Report.

Today, social security accounts for the largest portion of government spending. Welfare benefits can be split into three main groups:

contributory benefits	= where entitlement depends on paying National Insurance contributions, e.g. pensions
non-contributory benefits	= where entitlement does not depend on National Insurance contributions or means testing, e.g. health care
means-tested benefits	= where entitlement depends on an individual's financial circumstances, e.g. free school meals.

Although most people agree that that the state has some measure of responsibility for the welfare of vulnerable citizens, what this should mean in practice is a much more contentious issue. The demand for welfare is infinite, but resources are finite. So where is the line to be drawn? The traditional view is that the state should act as a 'safety net', guaranteeing a minimum supply of essential goods and services or a minimum money income to be spent on the essentials. But what is to count as 'essential'? Attitudes and expectations vary over time, e.g. household items like fridges and washing machines, once thought of as luxuries, are now generally regarded as essentials.

Those who favour greater state involvement argue that state provision makes it easier to guarantee uniform standards throughout the country and has the advantage of economies of scale. Those who favour less state involvement argue that state provision has a tendency towards inflexibility and restricts individual freedom – if only the freedom to do what you want with your own money. They also argue that it can contribute to a culture of 'dependency' where people come to rely on the state for more and more and no longer bother to try to provide for themselves or their families. It stifles personal initiative and the sense of achievement that can come from relying on yourself when times are difficult.

Should welfare benefits be available to all or targeted at the less well off? In principle, targeting would seem to make it easier to concentrate resources on those most in need. But in practice, it can be more expensive than it sometimes appears. Targeting is complex to introduce. It involves some kind of 'means testing' associated with a sense of social stigma and resulting in the reluctance of some people to claim the benefits they are entitled to. Making benefits universal is one way of guaranteeing take-up. It can also contribute to a sense of solidarity and common citizenship in society.

On the other hand, making benefits free to all may well increase the level of inequality in society. This brings into question the very purpose of social welfare. Is the role of the state simply to provide a 'safety net' for the vulnerable – no more and no less – or is it to help to create a more equal society through the redistribution of resources? Those who favour some form of redistribution are also likely to wish to outlaw parallel non-state provision of certain forms of social welfare, e.g. private education or medicine.

How is social security to be paid for? Some people favour a flat rate for all. Others prefer some form of sliding scale, ranging from nothing to the full cost of the service. How should benefits be paid: in cash, through tax relief, in the form of directly provided services, in grants or subsidies to voluntary organisations? In many ways, this is a practical question, but it is also a moral and political one. To what extent should individual citizens be free to decide for themselves how their benefits are to be spent?

In recent years, debate has focused on the day-to-day running of welfare services – in particular, the role of voluntary organisations and private enterprise. Public services can be 'contracted out' to commercial companies while retaining state control through regulation and inspection. This raises the question of whether it is right that private companies should profit from public service. Alternatively, elements of the free market, such as consumer choice and competition, can be introduced into public service provision in the form of 'internal markets'. Supporters argue that this increases efficiency, but critics claim it undermines the ethos of 'public service' associated with public welfare and alters the status of users – no longer fellow citizens but consumers.

The central activity in this unit revolves around an extract from an imaginary travel journal in which the author describes an unusual system of social security found on one of the islands he visits. However, despite the apparent benefits, the islanders are far from satisfied with the system. This raises a number of questions.

- What sorts of social welfare should we expect the state to provide and what should individuals and their families be expected to provide for themselves?

- What role, if any, is there for voluntary organisations and private enterprise in this process?

- Should welfare benefits be available to all or should entitlement be dependent on a person's financial circumstances?

- How should benefits be paid for?

WHAT SHOULD THE STATE DO FOR US?

■ INTRODUCTION

This is a lesson about social welfare. In this lesson, you will learn about different sorts of welfare benefits, the ways in which they are organised and paid for, and how fair you think it is to expect the government to provide these.

■ STARTER

Citizens in need

In pairs, make a list of the types of citizen that you think are most in need in this country. Share your examples with the class and explain why you have chosen them. Whose duty is it to help citizens when they are in need? Why?

■ BEVERIDGE ISLAND

To help you think about this issue, read **Beveridge Island** (Student Sheet 13.1, p117).

1. As a class, think about reasons why the islanders are always complaining about the monkeys.

■ Why might they think the system is unfair? How many different reasons can you think of?

Suggested answers

- *every working adult has to pay the same regardless of income*
- *the unemployed should have to pay at least a token fee*
- *the government should not be telling citizens how to spend their money*
- *it takes away all initiative from people*
- *it discourages people from taking responsibility for themselves and others*
- *people should rely on themselves, not on payments from others*
- *it increases the gap between rich and poor*
- *people are getting monkeys who do not need them*
- *animals are not meant to be slaves.*

■ Do you think the system is unfair? If so, how would you make it fairer?

2. In small groups, look at the items on the Discussion Cards (Student Sheet 13.2, p118). Take a card in turn and decide, without discussing, whether you think it is something the government in our country should provide for citizens in:

- ■ ALL cases
- ■ SOME cases
- ■ NO cases.

Form three piles of cards accordingly. When you have used up all the cards, group members have an opportunity to question your decisions and, if the group agrees, move one or more of the cards to a different pile.

3. Share your decisions with the class and explain the reasoning behind them.

■ *PLENARY*

As a class, try to agree the sort of welfare benefits you think:

- ■ the government should provide for UK citizens
- ■ UK citizens should provide for themselves.

☐ BEVERIDGE ISLAND

Of all the peoples I visited on my travels, the most ungrateful were the inhabitants of Beveridge Island.

What was remarkable about the people on the island was the way they had trained the monkeys that lived there. Over the years, the Beveridge Islanders had trained monkeys to do many of the tasks that only human beings had been able to do.

All the monkeys were owned by the island government. The government arranged for a set number of monkeys to be given to each family every year. In return for this, people had to pay a set fee. The bigger the family, the more monkeys they got. Elderly people, pregnant women, the sick and the disabled were given extra monkeys. Every working adult paid the same rate and people without a job paid nothing.

The range of activities carried out by the monkeys was quite amazing. They were able to do everything people needed — from the cradle to the grave! They cleaned and prepared food for the table, carried water, cared for the old and sick, and minded the children — female monkeys suckling the human babies. They worked outdoors, too, planting and harvesting crops, mining coal and precious metals, and labouring on building sites. Indeed, this free labour enabled some of the rich farmers, mine-owners and property builders to get even richer.

What a contrast this was to the olden times on the island. In those days, as I later discovered, people were frightened to become ill or grow old. Care was restricted to those who could afford it. There were no monkeys to help the out-of-work or disabled. Life expectancy was low and education virtually non-existent. Children went out to work almost as soon as they were able to walk so that their families might have enough to eat.

And were the inhabitants of Beveridge Island grateful for the monkeys? Not one bit! The miserable wretches did nothing but complain. Not one of the Islanders I spoke to said they thought the system was fair.

For the life of me, dear reader, I cannot understand how anyone should think that a system that brought such benefits in life could be unfair. **Can you?**

☐ DISCUSSION CARDS

Food	**Smoke detectors**
Houses	**Heating**
Pensions	**TV licences**
Hospitals	**Transport**
Schools	**Holidays**
Washing machines	**Furniture**
Child care	**Jobs**
Funerals	**Clothes**

☐ RESEARCH TASK 1

■ FREE SCHOOL MEALS

A report produced by the Child Poverty Action Group for the government shows that one in five children entitled to school meals are not taking them. They are afraid of teasing, name-calling and bullying from other children.

Free school meals are available to pupils if their parents are in receipt of income support or job seeker's allowance. In secondary schools, this usually means being given tokens on a weekly basis to buy a midday meal. Some schools still have separate queues for pupils using free meal tokens or make them wait until paying children have collected their meals.

Some people say this is not fair, especially as a poor diet is second only to smoking as a contributory factor to cancer and heart disease. The answer, they argue, is to make school meals free for all pupils.

1. What are the arguments for and against making school meals free for all pupils? How many different ones can you think of? What is your opinion on this issue?

2. Find out the current rate of income support and job seeker's allowance.

3. Find out which welfare benefits are 'universal', i.e. available to all citizens, regardless of their ability to pay.

4. Find out what is meant by 'workfare'.

5. The idea of a 'welfare state' became very popular in this country in the late 1940s following the publication of a report by the UK economist William Henry Beveridge, the 'Report on Social Insurance and Allied Services'. Find out the sorts of thing that this report recommended.

6. It has been estimated that on average each household in the UK receives about £80 a week in welfare benefits. There is a view that says that the government should pay the £80 directly to families so they can spend it as *they* think fit instead of having to claim specific benefits. Do you think this would be a good idea? Why or why not?

For information about welfare benefits in the UK, go to *www.jobcentreplus.gov.uk*
For the Beveridge Report, go to *http://cepa.newschool.edu/het/profiles/beveridge.htm*

☐ RESEARCH TASK 2

■ *THE VOLUNTARY SECTOR*

Voluntary organisations often meet needs that are not met by local councils or central government, e.g. Age Concern provides services for old people, ChildLine provides services for children.

There are thousands of different voluntary organisations. They work in different ways:

■ providing services directly, e.g. Barnardo's
■ speaking up for certain groups in society, e.g. Child Poverty Action Group
■ helping people to help themselves, e.g. Alcoholics Anonymous.

1. What do you think are the advantages and disadvantages for citizens when welfare is provided by the voluntary sector rather than the state?

2. Find out what different voluntary organisations are operating in the area where you live.

3. Carry out a small piece of research into a voluntary organisation that deals with an area of welfare you feel strongly about. How is it funded? What sort of needs does it try to meet? How does it go about this? Decide how you are going to present your findings. Investigate possible links you could make between the organisation and your school or college, e.g. work experience placements, visiting speakers, fundraising, publicity, and so on.

Politics

■ AIMS

This unit aims to help students to:

- identify a range of reasons for entering public life

- recognise some of the moral dilemmas that arise in public life

- reflect upon the characteristics of an effective politician.

■ CITIZENSHIP THEMES

- Central and local government

- The media's role in society

- Public services and how they are financed

- The rights and responsibilities of consumers

■ KEYWORDS

accountability	having to give an explanation for your actions
brief against	make information available to the press or the public in order to damage or undermine someone else
conflict of interest	having two or more different interests to serve, which clash with each other
fudge	dodge an issue by telling only part of the truth
hypocrisy	double standards, not practising what you preach
integrity	honesty, sticking to your principles
leak	make information available to the press or the public without letting your identity be widely known
lesser of evils	choosing the least worst option when faced with two or more courses of action, all of which have bad consequences
mixed motives	having more than one reason for doing something
moral courage	the courage to do what you believe to be right
pragmatic	acting on what is practically achievable rather than on principle

public interest	things that affect the general public, or that the general public has a right to know about or be involved in
sleaze	an atmosphere of corruption or dishonesty
whistleblower	an informer

■ BACKGROUND

This unit is about political virtues, i.e. the qualities of character that are important in public life. The characteristics expected of political leaders vary according to the kind of government that is thought desirable. Ruthlessness and rule by fear may be valued in a dictatorship but are not the sort of qualities appropriate for a democracy.

Candidates for election need to appeal to a wide range of people if they are to be elected. If voters do not like the appearance or personality of a candidate, the candidate is unlikely to receive their vote. A politician's 'charisma' is often thought to be an important factor in whether they are elected. To a certain extent, this relates to how politicians perform in public, e.g. their ability at public speaking. It also relates to how they are perceived and depicted by the media.

Beyond this lies the question of the sort of moral virtues we expect of our elected representatives. Public life presents politicians with a wide range of moral dilemmas, not least how best to use the tremendous amount of power that the electorate has invested in them. In times of war, this can even mean the power of life or death over both their citizens and citizens of other countries in the world. Politicians often have to face conflicts of interest: between what is in the public interest and what is good for their political careers. They have access to information that the electorate is not aware of and face the constant dilemma of what should be made public and what should be kept secret.

The committee of inquiry on 'Standards in Public Life' (Nolan committee) laid down seven principles of public life that now guide the behaviour of those holding public office in the UK, including local government. They are:

selflessness	=	decisions to be taken solely in the public interest
integrity	=	not to place yourself under financial obligations to outsiders who might influence you
objectivity	=	decisions on public issues to be made on merit
accountability	=	being accountable for actions and inactions
openness	=	decisions to be made as openly as possible

| honesty | = | a duty to declare private interests |
| leadership | = | these principles to be promoted by example. |

The central activity in this unit is a story about a sister and a brother who both rise to prominence in public life in their local town. Katerina becomes town mayor and her brother, Stefan, an influential doctor. Stefan discovers that infectious waste is seeping into the town's crumbling water pipes and making people ill. The pipes supply the local factory – the only real source of employment in the town – with 'health-giving' spring water that it bottles and sells throughout the country. When Stefan sends a report on the dangerous condition of the town's water supply to Katerina, the mayor, she tries to persuade him to suppress it.

The story, loosely based on Ibsen's play of the same name, explores some of the difficulties of being in public life. It shows how involvement in political life often means having to find a balance between conflicting social duties and interests, including one's own personal self-interest. It helps students to develop a wider understanding of reasons why people go into politics, and to become more able to empathise with the role of the professional politician in the difficult decisions he or she has to make.

At the heart of the story lie important questions. What are legitimate motives for going into public life? What qualities of character are important in public life? Are the values we think ought to be brought to bear in public life the same as those we think should apply to personal encounters in private life, or different? In other words, do good people make good politicians, or can being a good person be a disqualification for public life?

Unit 14 WHAT MAKES A GOOD POLITICIAN?

■ INTRODUCTION

This is a lesson about the sort of qualities people look for in a good politician. In this lesson, you will learn about different reasons why people become politicians, about some of the difficulties of being a politician, and about what you think makes a good politician.

■ STARTER

Why do you think someone wants to be a politician? In pairs, write down as many different reasons as you can think of. Briefly share some of your ideas with the rest of the class.

Suggested answers

- *to make money*
- *to be famous*
- *to be liked*
- *to boss other people around*

- *believes in a cause*
- *to do good/help other people*
- *family members are/were also politicians*
- *a mixture of motives.*

■ ENEMY OF THE PEOPLE

To help you think about this more, read the story **Enemy of the People** (Student Sheet 14.1, pp126–7).

1. As a class, think about the story you have just read. What reasons might Katerina have for wanting her brother to keep quiet about the report? How many different ones can you think of?

Suggested answers

- *people will not buy the bottled water and many jobs will be lost, the factory may even have to close down*
- *Katerina would have to admit to making a wrong decision*
- *she may lose her job as mayor*
- *she may find herself in trouble with the law if she is found responsible for people's deaths*
- *personal rivalry between herself and her brother.*

2. In small groups, imagine what you would say if you were in Katerina's position. Look at the suggestions on the Discussion Cards (Student Sheet 14.2, p128) and put together a response using the prompts on the cards – as many or as few as you wish. Develop some arguments to support the response you have chosen.

You may wish to make this a written exercise by asking students to draft a press release that Katerina might put out.

3. Discuss your ideas with the class. Do you think it is right for Katerina to try to keep the report quiet? Why or why not?

Suggested answers

YES:

- *to prevent panic*
- *to prevent jobs being lost*
- *it is not definite that the poisoning is being caused by the infected material in the water*
- *even if the pipes are replaced, people might never trust the water again*
- *Katerina might lose her job and be replaced by someone much worse for the town*
- *it is the lesser of evils.*

NO:

- *the public have a right to know*
- *the problem with the water might go on and on*
- *more people might get ill and die*
- *if Katerina is found out, the public will never trust her again*
- *the report will get out sooner or later anyway.*

4. Do you think there are times when it is right for politicians to lie? If so, when? Discuss your thinking with the class.

Suggested answers

- *national security, e.g. to protect lives*
- *about their personal lives, e.g. to protect family members.*

■ *PLENARY*

In pairs, fill in the questionnaire about the qualities you would look for in a politician (Student Sheet 14.3, p129). Compare your answers with the class. Has anyone's ideas on this changed since the beginning of the lesson? If so, how?

☆ □ ENEMY OF THE PEOPLE

Katerina and Stefan grew up together in a small country town. Apart from both having blond hair, it was difficult to tell they were sister and brother. Katerina was outgoing and noisy, and always in trouble. Stefan was quiet and less confident. He was jealous of the way Katerina made friends easily.

Stefan went to university to train as a doctor. Katerina left school as soon as she could and got a job in the local bottling factory. The factory employed most of the people in the town. It bottled local water and sold it all over the country. The water was famous for its health-giving properties.

Katerina was popular with the other workers in the factory – though not with the owner – and soon got involved in factory politics. She got a name for standing up for the rights of younger workers. At 21, she put her name forward in the election for town mayor. To the horror of many older people, she got enough votes to win and became the youngest mayor in the town's history.

Becoming mayor was a like a dream come true for Katerina. She loved being the centre of attention. She called herself 'The People's Friend'. She had lots of ideas about how to make the town better for people, especially for young people.

When Stefan finished his training, he came back to his hometown to work as a doctor. By now, he was married with two small children. His family was proud of him and the job he did, but he still felt a little in his sister's shadow.

Then something happened that was to affect Stefan and Katerina's relationship for ever. People began to turn up at Stefan's surgery with quite serious cases of poisoning. Many of them were too ill to work and were struggling to find enough money to live on. A number of older people died, but it was not clear whether it was because of the illness or not. Nor was it clear what the long-term effects of the illness would be on younger people.

On investigation, Stefan discovered that infected waste material was seeping into the local water supply. The water pipes were old and crumbling. The whole system was falling apart.

Stefan sent a report to his sister, the mayor. Katerina sent a note back to the surgery immediately: 'Don't breathe a word of this to anyone. If the news gets out, we'll *all* be ruined.'

It turned out that Katerina had known the water pipes would need replacing ever since she became mayor, but she felt that spending money in other ways, especially on schools, was more important in the short term.

She said to Stefan, 'If you "forget" about the report, I'll get the works department to start replacing the pipes as soon as they can, okay?'

Stefan was angry. He said he could not 'forget' about the report: 'The public has a right to know.'

Two days later, Katerina took a phone call from the editor of the local newspaper. He had heard a rumour that there was a problem with the town's water supply and this was behind the recent cases of poisoning. He wanted to know if the rumour was true.

Katerina took a deep breath. What was she to say now?

☐ DISCUSSION CARDS

Thank the newspaper for letting you know	**Say that if you looked into *every* rumour you heard, you would never get anything done**
Say that if there is anything wrong with the water supply, it is because the previous mayor allowed the water pipes to get into such a bad state	**Say you are aware the water pipes do need replacing and you are sorting this out as quickly as you can**
Promise you will look into the rumour and see if there is any truth in it	**Admit you have made a mistake**
Say you are thinking about the people who are ill and their families, and hope they will soon be better	**Say you are aware that the water pipes do need replacing but, as far as you know, this has nothing to do with the cases of poisoning in the town**
Say that the townspeople voted for you to do something for young people and by improving the schools that is what you have done	**Say you cannot win. If you had spent lots of money on the water supply, people would have complained that you had not spent any on schools**
Say that as mayor you had difficult decisions to make and, rightly or , wronglyyou made the decision to improve schools	**Say you are sorry**
Something else?	**Something else?**

□ QUESTIONNAIRE

Consider the following characteristics and decide how important you think they are in a politician. Try to put them into three categories: not important, important, very important.

	Not important	Important	Very important
Intelligence	□	□	□
Honesty	□	□	□
Good health	□	□	□
Courage	□	□	□
Good listener	□	□	□
A sense of humour	□	□	□
Good looks and dress sense	□	□	□
Trustworthiness	□	□	□
Good talker	□	□	□
Principles	□	□	□
Ability to inspire confidence in others	□	□	□
Willingness to put others first	□	□	□
A desire to improve society	□	□	□
A thick skin	□	□	□
Ability to see all sides of an argument	□	□	□
Good actor	□	□	□
Desire to succeed	□	□	□
Good judgement	□	□	□

☐ RESEARCH TASK 1

■ *LEO'S JAB*

The Prime Minister, Tony Blair, has constantly refused to tell the public whether his youngest son, Leo, has been given an MMR injection.

MMR is a three-in-one vaccine that protects children from measles, mumps and rubella. Some people claim that the vaccine is dangerous and causes autism and bowel disease. They say that it is much safer to have three separate injections.

The government disagrees, quoting research from health service experts saying that MMR is perfectly safe. It wants parents to take their children to have the MMR jab and is making it more difficult for them to have the three injections separately.

1. Do you think the public have a right to know whether Leo has had the MMR jab? What are the arguments for and against this?

2. Find out about the Official Secrets Act. What sorts of information does this law require politicians to keep secret?

3. Find out what is meant by a 'D' Notice.

4. Carry out your own survey into the kind of information that people think they have a right to know about their politicians.

Topics you might choose to ask about include:

- ■ how much politicians earn
- ■ whether politicians have ever taken drugs
- ■ where politicians' children go to school.

Decide who you are going to ask and how you are going to present your results.

For information about the Official Secrets Act, go to *www.ind.homeoffice.gov.uk* For general information about freedom of information, go to *www.cfoi.org.uk*

☐ RESEARCH TASK 2

■ *WHAT MAKES A GOOD STUDENT COUNCILLOR?*

Here are some things that student councillors say about their role:

■ 'It's quite hard to get things across to the teachers and you have to really push at it if you want things done.'

■ 'Getting together 12–14 people to sit down at the same time, have something to discuss, have people who fill all the supposed roles, is very difficult.'

■ 'There are two reasons why I initially joined. One, because I like to have a say in things that go on and I wanted to see things happen. But also, what I think is selfish, I could put it on my UCAS form and it was very helpful and got me five offers from universities.'

■ 'Basically, 90 per cent of the school isn't really bothered about the school parliament.'

■ 'Nobody really sort of notices what happens, they just take it for granted.'

■ 'Sometimes we don't actually agree with what the people have said, but still it is our duty to pass it on.'

Don Rowe, *The Business of Schools Councils*

1. What do you think makes a good student councillor? Make a list of the skills and qualities you think a student needs to be a good school or college councillor. How, if at all, are these different from what you would look for in a good politician?

2. Carry out your own investigation into reasons why someone becomes a student councillor. What conclusions can you draw from this? Decide how you might use your findings to improve the standard of representation in your own school or college council.

3. The UK Youth Parliament is a national body of democratically elected young people aged from 11–18. Find out what Members of the Youth Parliament (MYPs) do, how they are elected, and where they meet. Consider how you might present some of the issues important to students in your school or college to your local MYPs for consideration.

For information about the UK Youth Parliament, go to *www.ukyouthparliament.org.uk*

■ AIMS

This unit aims to help students to:

■ recognise some of the different sorts of question asked in political interviews

■ become familiar with some of the different ways in which politicians respond to questioning

■ reflect upon the fairness of the different tactics used in political interviews.

■ CITIZENSHIP THEMES

■ The media's role in society

■ Central and local government

■ KEY WORDS

ad hominem	argument that attacks a person's character rather than the point they are trying to make
cliché	a commonly-used expression that has lost its meaning through overuse
false dichotomy	being forced to choose between two options when other options are available
leading question	question worded in such a way that it tends to lead to a predetermined reply
loaded term	word or phrase used to direct people unconsciously to a particular point of view, e.g. 'swamping' of immigration
misrepresent	present a slanted or oversimplified version of someone's argument to make it easier to attack
rhetoric	art of using language to persuade or influence
soundbite	short, easy to remember, phrase or slogan
spin	twist news to favour a particular point of view

■ BACKGROUND

This unit is about the tactics used by journalists and politicians in political interviews. Politicians want to be in the news, but only if it puts them and their parties in a good light. They want voters to hear about their policies, think well of them, and vote for them in elections.

As a rule, however, there is little time for detailed discussion of policy in TV or radio interviews. Politicians have to use what little time they have to their best advantage. They also have to defend themselves in the face of the difficult sorts of question that journalists ask.

Political parties provide professional media training on what to do and what not to do in interviews. Sometimes a politician will only agree to take part in an interview if the questioning is restricted to certain subjects and a deal will be done on this prior to the interview taking place. Often, the information the politician is willing to share on an issue will be decided beforehand. So no matter what questions the interviewer actually asks, the politician will try to steer the interview around to what he or she has planned to say, i.e. remain 'on message'.

Politicians use a number of practical strategies to help them get the best out of an interview and fend off awkward lines of questioning. They include:

■ clichés, e.g. 'The fact of the matter…'

■ soundbites, e.g. 'Tough on crime, tough on the causes of crime…'

■ loaded terms, e.g. 'politically correct'.

The important thing is to:

■ not give simple 'yes' or 'no' answers

■ say something – anything is better than nothing

■ make sure you have the last say

■ end on a positive note.

The central activity in this unit involves the transcript of an imaginary TV interview with a politician on the subject of legislation relating to the smacking of children. The dialogue illustrates some of the different forms of questioning journalists use in political interviews and the ways in which politicians typically respond. The exercise not only helps students to identify some of the tactics that are used in political interviews, but also to reflect upon their fairness and appropriateness for public life in a democratic society.

WHY WON'T POLITICIANS ANSWER THE QUESTION? Unit 15

■ *INTRODUCTION*

This is a lesson about the way politicians behave in interviews. In this lesson, you will learn about some of the different sorts of question that are asked in political interviews, how politicians respond to them, and how fair you think their answers are.

■ *STARTER*

What sort of questions do you think it would be unfair to be asked at a job interview? Fill in the questionnaire on Student Sheet 15.1, p135.

■ *THE MAX PANN INTERVIEW*

Choose two volunteers to perform **The Max Pann Interview** (Student Sheet 15.2, pp136–137).

1. In pairs, think about the way that Max questions Eve.

■ What sort of tactics does he use?

Suggested answers
• *interrupting/not giving her enough time to answer*
• *repeating a question that has not been answered*
• *misrepresenting her case/twisting her words*
• *loaded terms, e.g. 'beating'*
• *personal questions, e.g. about her own children*
• *leading questions, e.g. 'Why the U-turn?'*
• *false dichotomy, e.g. being against or in favour of smacking*
• *dredging up the past, e.g. STOPP.*

■ Do you think Max's behaviour is fair? Why or why not?

2. Share your ideas with the class.

3. In small groups, think about the ways in which Eve responds to Max's questioning. Look at the information sheet on Top Tactics for Dealing with Awkward Questions (Student Sheet 15.3, p138). Which of these tactics does Eve use? How many can you find?

Suggested answers

- *attack the question – 'that kind of question just trivialises...'*
- *attack the questioner – 'what century are you living in?'*
- *defuse the question – 'the question is not whether I smack...'*
- *ignore the question – 'the truth is that this government...'*
- *invoke secrecy – 'you can't expect me to give a definite commitment'*
- *ramble on – at the end of the interview*
- *buy time – 'let me be absolutely clear...'.*

Look back at your copy of the Max Pann Interview (Student Sheet 15.2, pp136–137). Mark the different tactics with a highlighter pen and label them accordingly.

4. Compare your ideas with the class.

5. In groups of four, try to imagine what was going on inside Max and Eve's heads privately during the interview, e.g. their feelings about the way the interview was going, the tactics the other was using, how they were planning to respond, who was in control of the interview, their plans for the interview, etc. Write these private thoughts into the interview in the form of two more speaking parts: one for Max's internal self, and one for Eve's.

6. Perform the revised interview for the class. Who do you think is actually controlling this interview – Max or Eve? Why?

■ *PLENARY*

On your own, reflect upon this issue:

Are there questions it would be *wrong* for a politician to answer? If so, what kind and why?

Suggested answers

- *questions about national security*
- *questions about the politician's family or private life*
- *questions that if answered may cause unnecessary public upset/panic*
- *questions that would take too long to answer in the time available*
- *questions that if answered may damage his/her party*
- *leading questions that might incriminate him/her.*

Go round the class and compare your ideas.

☐ FAIR AND UNFAIR QUESTIONS

Imagine you were asked the following questions at a job interview. Which of them do you think are fair questions to be asked and which are unfair? Why?

	Fair	Unfair	Reason
What makes you think you would be good at this job?			
Are you prepared to work weekends?			
Have you got many friends?			
Have you ever been in trouble with the law?			
Have any members of your family ever been in trouble with the law?			
What experience have you got of this sort of work?			
How old are you?			
What do you think about the other candidates for the job?			

What do you think is the best thing to do if you are asked an unfair question?

☐ THE MAX PANN INTERVIEW

Max: Good evening. I have with me tonight Eve Hayder MP. She'll be talking about her party's response to the government's plan to outlaw the smacking of children.

[turning to studio guest] So you want to be known as the party that encourages parents to beat their children, Ms Hayder?

Eve: What we say in our discussion paper has nothing to do with beating children…

Max: *[interrupting]* You're *against* smacking, then? I thought you were in favour of it?

Eve: What we are in favour of, Max, is parents having the *right* to decide for themselves whether they should smack their children. It is a million miles away from beating.

Max: And do you smack your own children?

Eve: The question is not whether or not I smack my own children, but whether parents should be allowed the freedom to decide for themselves, instead of being told what to do by the state.

Max: Do you smack your own children?

Eve: If you don't mind me saying so, Max, that kind of question just trivialises the debate. The important question is whether the government should be allowed to dictate to parents what they should and should not do.

Max: So it's all right to tell other people how to behave with their children but you're not prepared to say how you behave with your own?

Eve: We've made it perfectly clear how we stand on this issue. It's not a matter of telling other people how to behave…

Max:	*[interrupting]* So I can take it you *don't* smack your own children, then?
Eve:	You can take nothing of the sort. The fact of the matter is that the present government is about to take away a basic right that parents have had from the beginning of time: the right to administer a mild smack to a naughty child.
Max:	Am I correct in thinking that you are the same Eve Hayder who in the 1980s was a leading supporter of STOPP? For the benefit of viewers who might not know, STOPP was a pressure group that campaigned against corporal punishment in schools.
Eve:	Max, what century are you living in? I'm here to answer questions that matter to people living in the twenty-first century, not about the dim and distant past.
Max:	One minute you were campaigning against corporal punishment, the next campaigning in favour of it? Why the U-turn?
Eve:	You're really scraping the bottom of the barrel with this line of questioning, Max. This is not what the viewers want to hear. They want to know about our policies and what we plan to do when we come to power.
Max:	So if the government bans the right to smack, your party would bring it back if – or when – you came to power?
Eve:	The reality of the situation is that the present government is doing it's very best to undermine parents and undermine the family. We are – and always have been – the party that supports parents and supports families. When we come to power, we will do everything we can to strengthen the rights of parents to bring up their children in a disciplined and positive way.
Max:	You haven't answered the question. Would you or would you not bring it back?
Eve:	With the best will in the world, you can't expect me to make a definite commitment to a policy that is still at the discussion stage. No opposition spokesman would do that.
Max:	So you've no idea what you would do if you were in government, then?
Eve:	*[sensing time is running out]* The truth is that this government is a shambles. One by one it is taking away all the basic freedoms that citizens have traditionally enjoyed in this country. Let me be absolutely open and honest with you. Our message is clear and simple. We are the party of the family and we will do everything in our power to support families in this country.
Max:	I'm sorry. That's all we've got time for. Thank you, Eve Hayder.

☐ TOP TACTICS FOR DEALING WITH AWKWARD QUESTIONS

1. Attack the question

For example, 'That's a rather trivial question. I think a more important question is...'

2. Attack the questioner

For example, 'If you had ever been in government, you would know full well that...'

3. Defuse the question

For example, if questioned about the results of an opinion poll that is not in your favour, say, 'I never pay any attention to opinion polls.'

4. Ignore the question

Simply carry on with your previous answer, or move on to a different topic, as though the question had never been asked.

5. Invoke secrecy

Explain that you cannot answer the question without giving away information that should be kept secret, for example, about the tactics your party intends to use in the run-up to the next election.

6. Buy time

Keep talking so no one will remember the question or be able to tell whether you have answered it or not, for example, by speaking in clichés, such as 'the fact of the matter...' The longer you talk, the fewer awkward questions you can get asked.

☐ RESEARCH TASK 1

■ *RECORD AN INTERVIEW*

Record a TV interview with a politician.

Tony Blair being interviewed by TV presenter David Frost.

1. Draw up a grid that you can use to identify and record the sort of tactics used by the interviewer and interviewee, e.g. clichés, attacking the question, etc., no more than one side of A4.

2. Watch the recording and note down your findings.

3. Compare your findings with others in the class and discuss what you can learn from this exercise.

☐ RESEARCH TASK 2

■ *DEMON EYES*

One of the most famous political advertising campaigns in recent years was run by the Conservative Party. It featured a picture of Tony Blair that had been altered to give him a pair of evil-looking demon eyes.

This was a clear example of negative advertising. Instead of focusing on the positive aspects of their own party, the Conservatives chose to run a negative campaign against their leading opponents, the Labour Party.

Negative political campaigning is not unusual. However, opinion is divided as to how effective it is. Much depends upon whether a campaign is believable or not. If it is believable, it may well work. If it is unbelievable, the campaign may have the opposite effect from the one you intended and drive voters into the arms of your opponents.

1. Find some more examples of political advertising. Classify these in terms of whether you regard them as positive or negative campaigning.

2. Watch an interview with a politician or a TV programme that features politicians talking, e.g. *Question Time*. Calculate the amount of time the politicians spend talking about their own party and the amount of time they spend criticising other parties.

3. Some people say that there is a difference between a 'reasonable attack' on another party and a 'slagging campaign'. Do you agree? If so, where would you draw the line?

4. What is meant by 'propaganda'? Illustrate your answer with some examples.

■ AIMS

This unit aims to help students to:

■ develop an understanding of the concept of ideology

■ become familiar with a range of political beliefs and ideologies

■ learn about the sorts of political beliefs and ideologies that influence politics in the UK today.

■ CITIZENSHIP THEMES

■ Central and local government

■ Parliamentary and other forms of government

■ Legal and human rights and responsibilities.

■ KEYWORDS

authoritarian	emphasising strict control and obedience to authority
ideology	system of beliefs and values that inspires people to take certain forms of action
libertarian	emphasising the freedom of the individual to live with as little interference from the state as possible
manifesto	a statement of policies and aims that a political party promises to do if it is elected as the next government
opposition party	political party that has not been elected to government
policy	plan of action
political party	group of people with a particular set of political beliefs, formed to elect representatives to government
values	what you think is right or wrong, good or bad, important or unimportant in life

■ BACKGROUND

This unit is about political beliefs and ideologies. Political beliefs can be classified in different ways. Traditionally, political views have been measured on a 'left-wing'/'right-wing' spectrum. The terms go back to the seating arrangements in the French National Assembly of 1789.

Broadly speaking, if you have left-wing views, you will be against inherited privilege and in favour of equality, democracy and government control of public services. If you have right-wing views, you will be against government control of public services and in favour of the freedom of the individual, private property, strong laws, custom and tradition. Where a person or a party is on this spectrum tells you how far to the 'left' or to the 'right' their political views are.

Another way of classifying political views is in terms of the kinds of political ideology on which they are based. A political ideology is a system of beliefs and values that inspires people to take certain forms of political action. Political ideologies are complex. Typically, they combine beliefs about:

■ human nature

■ nature of society

■ what is wrong with society

■ how this can be put right.

Traditionally, political parties in the UK have tended to align themselves with a particular ideology, e.g. the Labour Party with socialism, and the Conservative Party with conservatism. It would be wrong, however, to identify political parties with any one ideology. Parties are always changing and are able to accommodate a number of different strands of ideological thinking at the same time. Also, ideologies themselves change over time; old ones decline and new ones are developed – hence the rise, for example, of environmentalism.

For these reasons, some commentators have argued that political views are better classified in other ways; for example, in terms of where they lie on an 'authoritarian'/'libertarian' spectrum. Authoritarians favour state legislation on issues such as drugs and abortion, whereas libertarians believe that citizens should be able to live with as little interference from the state as is possible.

The central activity in this unit involves a comparison of the different beliefs underlying speeches by Martin Luther King and Malcolm X. Both were involved in the civil rights movement in the US in the 1960s, but each had different views of what equality meant and how it could be achieved. This leads on to a consideration of the different strands of ideological thinking that characterise contemporary UK political parties and their policies. Students are given descriptions of these three major political ideologies – liberalism, conservatism and socialism – and asked to match them with a range of policies promoted in the party

manifestos for the 2001 UK general election. This raises the questions, are all political views equally valid or are there some political views that are unacceptable in a democratic society?

This is one of the most challenging units in the pack and is only likely to be suitable for use with high-achieving Key Stage 4 or Key Stage 5 students.

WHAT DO POLITICAL PARTIES STAND FOR? Unit 16

■ *INTRODUCTION*

This is a lesson about political beliefs. In this lesson, you will learn about different kinds of political belief, the sort of beliefs that politicians have in this country, and where you stand on these beliefs yourself.

■ *STARTER*

Where do you stand on political issues? Fill in the questionnaire (Student Sheet 16.1, p145). Compare your answers with others. What does this exercise tell you about the sort of beliefs held in your class?

> You may wish to do this as a physical exercise with students locating themselves along a line to express their views.

TWO SPEECHES

Divide the class into two halves: one half reads Martin Luther King's speech (Student Sheet 16.2, p146) and the other reads Malcolm X's speech (Student Sheet 16.3, p147).

1. Form a pair with someone who has read the same speech as you. Think about the ideas behind the words you have just read. What do they tell you about the speaker's beliefs?

Suggested answers

MARTIN LUTHER KING BELIEVES:
- *black people are treated unjustly/suffer from segregation and discrimination/are poorer than other members of society*
- *they should be given freedom/equal opportunities/civil rights/right to vote*
- *something needs to be done about this quickly*
- *justice should not be obtained through physical violence*
- *it needs white people and black people to work together*
- *all people are created equal*
- *they should not give up until a better society is achieved*
- *things will get better.*

MALCOLM X BELIEVES:
- *black people are treated unfairly in society*
- *white people are responsible for this*
- *a revolution is going to take place*
- *white people will be punished by God for what they have done to black people*
- *violence is justified in self-defence*
- *white people have to be shocked to their senses*
- *black people and white people are better apart – and integration is wrong.*

2. Share your ideas with the class and compare your findings. On what things do Martin Luther King and Malcolm X agree or disagree?

3. Swap speeches with someone else and form a small group of people with the same new speech. Think carefully about the different sorts of belief underlying the words in the speech you have now got. You may wish to note down your thinking on Student Sheet 16.4, p148. What sorts of thing does the speaker believe about:

   ■ human beings
   ■ how human beings should live
   ■ what needs changing in society
   ■ how these changes can be achieved?

4. Read the information sheet on Three Political Ideologies (Student Sheet 16.5, p149).

5. In small groups, look at the Policy Statements (Student Sheet 16.6, p150). Each of these was made by one of the political parties contesting the 2001 UK general election. Sort the cards into three groups according to the kind of political beliefs you think they most closely reflect:

   ■ liberal
   ■ conservative
   ■ socialist.

Develop some arguments to support your choice.

6. Discuss your ideas with the class. Do you know which political party was responsible for each of these policies?

Answers:

1. Conservative	9. Conservative
2. Liberal Democrat	10. Green Party
3. Conservative	11. Labour
4. Scottish National Party	12. Liberal Democrat
5. Liberal Democrat	13. Liberal Democrat
6. Green Party	14. Scottish National Party
7. Labour	15. Conservative
8. Conservative	16. Green Party

■ *PLENARY*

Which of the three political ideologies would you say most reflects your political views? Write down your answer and your reasons for thinking this. Compare your thinking with others in the class.

You may wish to ask students to form three groups in different parts of the room to do this, then ask why they have joined the group they have.

☐ WHERE DO YOU STAND?

Consider the following statements and circle the response that you think most closely reflects your view, with 1 being 'strongly agree' and 10 being 'strongly disagree'.

1.   People who get into trouble with the law have only themselves to blame.   1 2 3 4 5 6 7 8 9 10

2.   All citizens should have an equal say in the running of society.   1 2 3 4 5 6 7 8 9 10

3.   The sooner we get rid of the royal family, the better.   1 2 3 4 5 6 7 8 9 10

4.   To get a fairer society, you sometimes have to resort to violence.   1 2 3 4 5 6 7 8 9 10

5.   All drugs should be legalised.   1 2 3 4 5 6 7 8 9 10

6.   The death penalty should be reintroduced for serial murderers.   1 2 3 4 5 6 7 8 9 10

7.   Human beings are basically good if you give them a chance.   1 2 3 4 5 6 7 8 9 10

8.   People should rely on themselves more and rely on the government less.   1 2 3 4 5 6 7 8 9 10

9.   Too much money is in too few hands in this country.   1 2 3 4 5 6 7 8 9 10

10.   We are all responsible for one another in society.   1 2 3 4 5 6 7 8 9 10

☐ MARTIN LUTHER KING

"Five score years ago, a great American, in whose symbolic shadow we stand, signed the Emancipation Proclamation…

But 100 years later, we must face the tragic fact that the Negro is still not free…

When the architects of our republic wrote the magnificent words of the Constitution and the Declaration of Independence, they were signing a promissory note to which every American was to fall heir. This note was a promise that all men would be guaranteed the inalienable rights of life, liberty, and the pursuit of happiness.

It is obvious today that America has defaulted on this promissory note insofar as her citizens of colour are concerned…

Let us not seek to satisfy our thirst for freedom by drinking from the cup of bitterness and hatred…

We must not allow our creative protest to degenerate into physical violence…

The marvellous new militancy which has engulfed the Negro community must not lead us to distrust of all white people, for many of our white brothers, as evidenced by their presence here today, have come to realise that their destiny is tied up with our destiny and their freedom is inextricably bound to our freedom. We cannot walk alone…

We cannot be satisfied as long as the Negro's basic mobility is from a smaller ghetto to a larger one. We can never be satisfied as long as a Negro in Mississippi cannot vote and a Negro in New York believes he has nothing for which to vote…

I have a dream that one day this nation will rise up and live out the true meaning of its creed: 'We hold these truths to be self-evident: that all men are created equal'…that one day on the red hills of Georgia the sons of former slaves and the sons of former slave owners will be able to sit down together at a table of brotherhood…that one day even the state of Mississippi, a desert state, sweltering with the heat of injustice and oppression, will be transformed into an oasis of freedom and justice…that my four children will one day live in a nation where they will not be judged by the colour of their skin but by the content of their character.

I have a dream today…"

☐ MALCOLM X

and will be the victims of God's divine wrath.

The war of Armageddon has already started…God is using his many weapons… Allah controls all things and he is using all methods to begin to wipe the devils off the planet.

When you've got some coffee that's too black, which means it's too strong, what do you do? You integrate it with cream…But if you pour too much cream in it, you won't even know you ever had coffee. It used to be hot, it becomes cool. It used to be strong, it becomes weak.

Segregation is that which is forced upon inferiors by superiors. Separation is done voluntarily by two equals. The Negro schools in the Negro community are controlled by whites…the economy of the Negro community is controlled by whites…Muslims who follow the Honorable Elijah Muhammad are as much against segregation as we are against integration. We are against segregation because it is unjust and we are against integration because it is a false solution to a real problem.

Our religion teaches us to be intelligent. Be peaceful, be courteous, obey the law, respect everyone; but if someone lays a hand on you, you send him to the cemetery.

I say that the common enemy is the white man.

It is criminal to teach a man not to defend himself when he is the constant victim of brutal attacks.

I'm an extremist. The black race…is in extremely bad condition."

"A new world order is in the making, and it is up to us to prepare ourselves that we take our rightful place in it.

At the bottom of the social heap is the black man in the big-city ghetto. He lives night and day with the rats and the cockroaches and drowns himself with alcohol and anaesthetises himself with dope to try and forget where and what he is.

We Muslims believe that the white race, which is guilty of having oppressed and exploited and enslaved our people here in America, should

☐ WHAT DOES HE BELIEVE?

What sort of things does the speaker believe about:

1. Human beings?

_____

_____

_____

_____

2. How human beings should live?

_____

_____

_____

_____

3. What needs changing in society?

_____

_____

_____

_____

4. How these changes can be achieved?

_____

_____

_____

_____

☐ THREE POLITICAL IDEOLOGIES

Liberalism

Liberalism emphasises the freedom of the individual. Liberals tend to believe that human beings naturally know what is good for them and should be free to decide for themselves what they do with their lives. They value tolerance, open-mindedness and protection of individual's rights. They think that central government today has too much control over people's lives and would like to see fewer rules and regulations and more opportunities for decisions to be taken locally.

Conservatism

Conservatism emphasises traditional institutions and ways of doing things. Conservatives tend to believe that although human beings are naturally motivated by self-interest, they do not always know what is good for themselves in the long run and need strong and wise leadership from the top. They value authority, law and order, private property and love for one's country. They think that the traditional authority structures that held society together – families, school, churches – are being undermined today. They would like to see a return to traditional values, greater rewards for private enterprise and more emphasis on people taking responsibility for themselves, their families and their communities, instead of relying on the government.

Socialism

Socialism emphasises equality. Socialists tend to believe that human beings are naturally co-operative and will act unselfishly in the interests of other people if given a chance. They value common ownership and joint effort. They think that society today is divided along lines of class and too much power is in the hands of the wealthy and privileged. They would like to see more power in the hands of the people, a redistribution of resources from the better-off to the less well-off and the benefits of social life – food, medicine, education, leisure – made available to everybody on equal terms.

☐ POLICY STATEMENTS

1. Keep the pound.

2. Free NHS dental and eye checks to be restored for all adults.

3. Local referendums before large increases in council tax.

4. Free daily fruit for all children in primary schools.

5. 50 per cent top rate of tax on earnings over £100,000.

6. A guaranteed income for every citizen.

7. Tougher punishments for crime.

8. Cut fuel tax by 6p per litre.

9. Remove the tax penalty on private medical insurance.

10. Increase support to women choosing home births.

11. Give more freedom to successful schools.

12. Extended prison education programmes.

13. Abolish university tuition fees.

14. End the so-called 'postcode treatment' of patients within the National Health Service.

15. Transfer power from central government to local councils.

16. Legalise cannabis for personal use at home.

☐ RESEARCH TASK 1

■ *WHERE DO PEOPLE STAND?*

Whether they realise it or not, everyone has political beliefs of one kind or another.

1. Using the information sheet on **Three Political Ideologies** (Student Sheet 16.5, p149), devise your own questionnaire to test which of these three political ideologies most informs people's thinking in your school, college or neighbourhood.

2. Decide which groups of people you want to ask and how you are going to present your results.

3. Research **one** of the following political ideologies and write a short piece describing its main features:

   ■ nationalism
   ■ fascism
   ■ anarchism
   ■ communism.

   With which political parties – in the UK or abroad, now or in the past – has the political ideology you have chosen been associated?

4. Choose one of the major UK political parties and investigate what ideological differences, if any, there are between its members.

☐ RESEARCH TASK 2

■ INCITING RACIAL HATRED OR FREEDOM OF EXPRESSION?

Nazis in plan to target stadium

Members of the November 9th Society, the British Nazi Party, plan to distribute leaflets outside the National Hockey Stadium before Wimbledon's home debut in Milton Keynes.

Some 9,000 fans are expected to pack the venue for Saturday's fixture and November 9th Society leader Kevin Quinn believes football crowds would be the ideal recruiting ground.

Up to 12 local members of the society will be handing out a four- to eight-page 'football comic' bearing the organisation's name and website address. 'The leaflets will be purely football related,' said Quinn, from Bedford.

Graham Thorley, spokesman for Wimbledon FC, which has no fewer than 11 black players in its first team squad, said the organisation will not be welcome. 'We have not yet been approached by this organisation,' he said. 'But if any neo-Nazi group was to ask the club for permission to hand out leaflets, they would be refused. The whole of football supports the 'Kick It Out Campaign'. It is a major part of football and we are not about to do anything that adds to racial tension.'

The November 9th Society is named after *Kristallnacht*, the night in 1938 when the German government sanctioned an attack on Jewish citizens, breaking shop windows, burning synagogues, and beating, raping, arresting and murdering Jews. Members of the society do not believe in democracy but say they are proud to call themselves Nazis and follow Hitler's political beliefs.

Their policies include:

- limiting immigration to white people, with each immigrant having to swear loyalty to the idea of Great Britain remaining a white nation
- non-whites having their British passports and citizenship taken from them and being expelled from this country
- no non-whites to be allowed to call themselves British.

The Public Order Act 1986 makes it a criminal offence to 'incite' or 'stir up' racial hatred, that is, hatred against any group defined by colour, race, nationality or ethnic or national origins. This includes the use of written material and video or audio recordings. In fact, it is an offence just to possess 'racially inflammatory' material unless you are unaware of its contents.

Milton Keynes Citizen, 25 September 2003

---

1. What are the arguments for and against allowing the November 9th Society to distribute their leaflets at the stadium? How many different ones can you think of? What is your opinion?

2. Should political parties be allowed to campaign on any issues they like or should some issues be banned? Why or why not? Illustrate your answer with some examples.

3. Do you think there should be laws that ban inciting or stirring up hatred against other groups not covered in the Public Order Act? If so, which groups and why?

4. Find out about and compare the political beliefs of:

   - Kick It Out Campaign
   - British National Party.